FACTS AT YOUR FINGERTIPS

INTRODUCING CHEMISTRY
METALS

BROWN
BEAR
BOOKS

CONTENTS

Published by Brown Bear Books Limited

4877 N. Circulo Bujia
Tucson, AZ 85718
USA

and

First Floor
9-17 St. Albans Place
London N1 ONX
UK
www.brownreference.com

© 2010 The Brown Reference Group Ltd

Library of Congress Cataloging-in-Publication Data

Metals / edited by Graham Bateman.
    p. cm. — (Facts at your fingertips)
Includes index.
ISBN 978-1-936333-12-7 (library binding)
1. Metals. I. Bateman, Graham. II. Title. III. Series.

QD171.M474 2010
546'.31—dc22

                                          2010016431

ISBN-13 978-1-936333-12-7

Editorial Director: Lindsey Lowe
Project Director: Graham Bateman
Design Manager: David Poole
Designer: Steve McCurdy
Text Editor: Briony Ryles
Indexer: David Bennett
Children's Publisher: Anne O'Daly
Production Director: Alastair Gourlay

Printed in the United States of America

Picture Credits
Abbreviations: SS=Shutterstock; c=center; t=top; l=left; r=right.

Cover Images
Front: SS: Shemp R. Camp
Back: istockphoto: photointrigue

1 SS: Iwona Grodzka; 3 SS: Oleg-F; 4-5 SS: Stillfx; 6 Wikimedia
Commons: Sergai Lachinov; 7t SS: Mircea Bezergheanu; 7b SS:
Travis Manley; 10 Wikimedia Commons: Parent Gery; 11 SS:
Antonio Jorge Nunes; 12tl Wikimedia Commons: Søren Wedel
Nielsen; 12tr Wikimedia Commons: Søren Wedel Nielsen; 13 SS:
Aquariagirl 1970; 14 Wikimedia Commons: Noodle snacks; 16-17
SS: Iwona Grodzka;17 SS: Petoo; 18 NASA-JPL; 19 SS: St. Nick; 20-
21 SS: Ventin; 21 SS: Carlos E. Santa Maria; 22 SS: Antikainen; 23
SS: DonVictorio; 24 SS: Kotomiti; 25 SS: Sabine Kappel; 28
Wikimedia Commons: Swisstack; 30-31 SS: Kris Jacobs; 32
Wikimedia Commons: Yannick McCabe –Costa; 34-35 SS: Tankist
276; 36-37 SS: Lobke Peers; 38 Wikimedia Commons: Meutia
Chaerani/Indradi Soemardjan; 39 Wikimedia Commons: Tmv23
& dblay; 40 SS: Fernando Cortes; 41 SS: Shane White; 42 SS:
Vitaly Raduntsev; 43 SS: Inginsh; 45 SS: Nikita Rogul; 46 SS:
Ben44; 48 SS: Tomas Pavelka; 49t Photos. com; 49b Photos.com;
50 SS: Lee Prince; 51 SS: Fotocrisis; 53 SS: Oleg-F; 54-55 SS:
Ctpaul; 56 SS: Gontar; 57 SS: Maciej Olesky; 58-59 SS: John
Carnemolla; 59 Wikimedia Commons: Rama; 60 Wikimedia
Commons: U.S. Department of Energy; 61 NASA-KSC.

Artwork © The Brown Reference Group Ltd

*The Brown Reference Group Ltd has made every effort to trace
copyright holders of the pictures used in this book. Anyone having
claims to ownership not identified above is invited to contact The
Brown Reference Group Ltd.*

Facts at your Fingertips—Introducing Chemistry describes the essentials of chemistry from the fundamentals of atomic structure, through the periodic table, to descriptions of different types of reactions and the properties of elements, including industrial applications for chemical processes.

Metals starts by describing the history and characteristics of the periodic table—a simple chart that organizes all the elements according to the chemical and physical properties of their atoms. After a general description of the characteristics of metals, there follow detailed accounts of the metallic elements, arranged in related groups according to the periodic table. For each group, there are detailed descriptions of their atomic structure, reactivity, properties, discovery, sources, uses, and much more.

Numerous explanatory diagrams and informative photographs, detailed features on related aspects of the topics covered and the main scientists involved in the advancement of chemistry, and definitions of key "Science Words," all enhance the coverage. "Try This" features outline experiments that can be undertaken as a first step to practical investigations.

THE PERIODIC TABLE

The modern periodic table was devised by Russian chemist Dmitry Ivanovich Mendeleyev (1834-1907). New elements have since been added, but the basic structure of Mendeleyev's table remains the same.

Legend has it that Mendeleyev came up with the periodic table when he was playing a card game called solitaire. There is little historical evidence, however, to back up this account. It is clear that Mendeleyev arranged the table using a list of atomic masses produced in 1860 at a science meeting in Karlsruhe, Germany. Atomic mass is the sum of the number of protons and neutrons in an atom's nucleus. Mendeleyev believed that atomic mass was the most important property of an element, though we now know that elements are defined by their atomic number—the number of protons in an atom's nucleus.

It is likely that Mendeleyev came up with the periodic table while he was writing a textbook, *The Principles of Chemistry* (1868-1870). In this book, Mendeleyev grouped elements with similar physical and chemical properties. For example, he grouped the halogens (Group 17 elements) in one chapter and the alkali metals in another chapter.

Mendeleyev was grouping elements with the same valence. Valence is a measure of the number of bonds an atom can form with other atoms. Valence is determined by the number of electrons in the outer electron shell of an atom. Atoms share or transfer these outer electrons, forming chemical bonds with other atoms. The halogens have similar properties because they all have seven electrons in the outer electron shell, and they all readily accept one electron to form bonds with other elements. In contrast, the alkali metals share physical and chemical properties because they have just one electron in the outer electron shell, and they all readily donate the electron to form bonds with other elements.

As Mendeleyev tried to group similar elements, a pattern emerged. He arranged the 61 known elements in a chart in order of increasing atomic mass. Mendeleyev found that elements with the same valence appeared in the same columns of the chart.

WHAT'S IN A NAME?

There is no right or wrong way to spell Mendeleyev's name in English. In Russian, words are written using the Cyrillic alphabet, for which there is no literal English translation. Consequently, you might see Mendeleyev's name written as Mendelev, Mendeleev, Mendeleeff, or Mendelayev.

Lightbulbs typically contain the noble gas argon. The noble gases rarely react with other elements and so were the last group of elements to be discovered and the last group that was added to the periodic table.

Mendeleyev had outlined the basic structure of the periodic table. He published his findings in 1869 and produced a revised table in 1871 that placed the elements into eight groups.

Filling the gaps

One of Mendeleyev's great achievements was to move elements to new places in the chart despite upsetting the order suggested by atomic mass. In this way, he kept the order of elements by valence. Perhaps the greatest achievement, however, was to describe elements that had not yet been discovered. Mendeleyev was convinced of the natural order of the periodic table. His table, however, contained gaps, and Mendeleyev reasoned that these gaps must represent elements not yet discovered. He even predicted the physical and chemical properties of these elements.

One of these gaps occurred below aluminum in Mendeleyev's table and so he named it eka-aluminum (*eka* is Sanskrit for "one" and eka-aluminum is one place from aluminum in the periodic table). This element was discovered by French scientist Paul-Emile Lecoq de Boisbaudran (1838–1912) in 1875. He called it gallium in honor of his country (*Gallia* is the Latin name for France). In 1879, Swedish chemist Lars Frederick Nilson (1840–1899) discovered the element that Mendeleyev called eka-boron. Nilson named this element scandium in honor of Scandinavia. In 1886, German chemist Clemens Winkler (1838-1904) discovered Mendeleyev's eka-silicon. Winkler named it germanium in honor of Germany. In all cases, the physical and chemical properties of the new elements matched Mendeleyev's predictions.

A new group of gases

In 1895, English chemist John William Strutt, later Lord Rayleigh (1842-1919), and Scottish chemist William Ramsay (1852-1916) identified a gas that they called argon. The new element did not seem to fit anywhere in Mendeleyev's periodic table. Ramsay thought that similar gases to argon must exist and so set about trying to find them. In 1895, he produced helium. In 1898, he carried out further

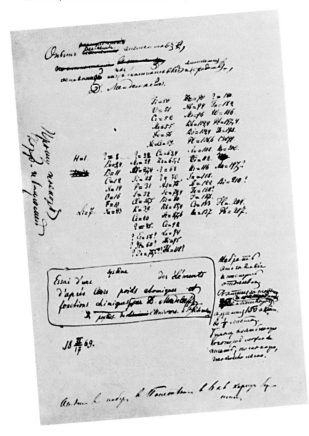

Dmitry Mendeleyev drew up the first version of his periodic table in 1869. He ordered the elements by atomic mass, leaving gaps for elements that he predicted would be discovered in the future.

SCIENCE WORDS

- **Atomic mass:** The number of protons and neutrons in a nucleus.
- **Atomic number:** The number of protons in an atom's nucleus.
- **Noble gases:** A group of gases that rarely react with other elements.
- **Valence:** A measure of the number of bonds an atom can form with other atoms.

research with English chemist Morris Travers (1872-1961) and together they identified neon, krypton, and xenon. Four years later, Mendeleyev revised his periodic table. He put the new group of gases in a group at the end of the periodic table. Chemists originally named this family of elements "inert gases," because they could not be made to react with other elements. Inert gases are now called noble gases because they do react in certain circumstances.

Atomic number

In 1911, New Zealand-born British physicist Ernest Rutherford (1871-1937) carried out an important experiment. This experiment revealed that the center of an atom consists of a dense, positively charged nucleus. Two years after Rutherford's discovery, English physicist Henry Moseley (1887-1915) used a machine called an electron gun to fire electrons at the atoms of different elements. He found that the elements gave off x-rays—high-energy radiation with short wavelengths. These x-rays had characteristics that depended on the number of protons in the nucleus. Moseley wrote down the proton number (now called atomic number) of many different elements. He then made a chart of all the known elements in order of increasing proton number. Following in Mendeleyev's footsteps, Moseley also left gaps in his chart, predicting the existence of two new elements. These missing elements were later discovered and are called

technetium and promethium. Moseley also corrected some of the errors associated with a table arranged by atomic mass.

The problem with atomic mass

Atomic mass is a measure of the number of protons and neutrons in the nucleus of an atom. The atoms of an element always contain the same number of protons, but they may have different numbers of neutrons. These different versions of atoms are called isotopes. Atomic number is the basic property on which the periodic table is best organized, not atomic mass. Fortunately for Mendeleyev, who did not know about protons and neutrons, atomic mass and atomic number increase roughly in proportion.

The last major change to the periodic table came in the middle of the 20th century. American physicist Glenn Seaborg (1912-1999) and his colleagues discovered 11 new elements with atomic numbers greater than that of uranium (atomic number 92). Seaborg rearranged the periodic table to accommodate these new elements.

Arc welding uses an electric current to produce a sparklike electric arc that fuses metals together by melting them. Argon is sometimes used in arc welding because it is an inert gas and so does not react with the molten metal, resulting in a more stable arc.

Scientists think that the blue color in aquamarine gemstones is caused by small quantities of scandium. Before scandium was discovered, Mendeleyev predicted its existence and physical properties using his periodic table.

READING THE PERIODIC TABLE

The periodic table organizes all the chemical elements into a simple chart according to the physical and chemical properties of their atoms.

The periodic table arranges elements in order of increasing atomic number. The rows are called periods and the columns are called groups. In general, elements in the same column have similar chemical properties. The electron arrangement in the atoms of elements determines the structure of the periodic table itself.

The basic order

The atomic number of an element is the number of protons in the nucleus of one atom of that element. A hydrogen atom always has one proton in its nucleus. The atomic number is 1, so hydrogen takes first place in the periodic table. A helium atom always has two protons in the nucleus. Its atomic number is 2, so it is second in the table, after hydrogen. A uranium atom always has 92 protons in its nucleus. The atomic number is 92 so uranium takes 92nd position.

Arranging elements in order of their atomic number eliminates the problems Mendeleyev had when he organized the elements in order of atomic mass. From left to right along a row of the periodic table, the atomic number rises by one whole unit for each element. Elements in lower rows have higher atomic numbers than elements above. Chemists can be

Transition metals

	Group 1	Group 2		Group 3	Group 4	Group 5	Group 6	Group 7	Group 8	Group 9
Period 1	1 **H** Hydrogen 1									
Period 2	3 **Li** Lithium 7	4 **Be** Beryllium 9								
Period 3	11 **Na** Sodium 23	12 **Mg** Magnesium 24								
Period 4	19 **K** Potassium 39	20 **Ca** Calcium 40		21 **Sc** Scandium 45	22 **Ti** Titanium 48	23 **V** Vanadium 51	24 **Cr** Chromium 52	25 **Mn** Manganese 55	26 **Fe** Iron 56	27 **Co** Cobalt 59
Period 5	37 **Rb** Rubidium 85	38 **Sr** Strontium 88		39 **Y** Yttrium 89	40 **Zr** Zirconium 91	41 **Nb** Niobium 93	42 **Mo** Molybdenum 96	43 **Tc** Technetium (98)	44 **Ru** Ruthenium 101	45 **Rh** Rhodium 103
Period 6	55 **Cs** Caesium 133	56 **Ba** Barium 137	Lanthanides	72 **Hf** Hafnium 179	73 **Ta** Tantalum 181	74 **W** Tungsten 184	75 **Re** Rhenium 186	76 **Os** Osmium 190	77 **Ir** Iridium 192
Period 7	87 **Fr** Francium 223	88 **Ra** Radium 226	Actinides	104 **Rf** Rutherfordium (263)	105 **Db** Dubnium (268)	106 **Sg** Seaborgium (266)	107 **Bh** Bohrium (272)	108 **Hs** Hassium (277)	109 **Mt** Meitnerium (276)

Atomic (proton) number
Chemical symbol

33 **As** Arsenic 75

Element name
Atomic mass

Rare-earth elements — Lanthanides — Actinides

Lanthanides

57 **La** Lanthanum 39	58 **Ce** Cerium 140	59 **Pr** Praseodymium 141	60 **Nd** Neodymium 144	61 **Pm** Promethium (145)
89 **Ac** Actinium 227	90 **Th** Thorium 232	91 **Pa** Protactinium 231	92 **U** Uranium 238	93 **Np** Neptunium (237)

Actinides

absolutely sure that there are no missing atomic numbers and no missing elements.

What does it show?

Each box of the periodic table represents one element. The box must show the element's atomic number, its name, and its chemical symbol. Aside from this, there are no strict rules. The atomic mass of the element is usually included, since it reflects the history of the periodic table. Some versions may have up to 20 data

ACTINIDES

NOBLE GASES

NONMETALS

METALLOIDS

HYDROGEN

ALKALI METALS

ALKALINE-EARTH METALS

METALS

LANTHANIDES

Group 18

			Group 13	Group 14	Group 15	Group 16	Group 17	2 **He** Helium 4
			5 **B** Boron 11	6 **C** Carbon 12	7 **N** Nitrogen 14	8 **O** Oxygen 16	9 **F** Fluorine 19	10 **Ne** Neon 20
Group 10	Group 11	Group 12	13 **Al** Aluminum 27	14 **Si** Silicon 28	15 **P** Phosphorus 31	16 **S** Sulfur 32	17 **Cl** Chlorine 35	18 **Ar** Argon 40
28 **Ni** Nickel 59	29 **Cu** Copper 64	30 **Zn** Zinc 65	31 **Ga** Gallium 70	32 **Ge** Germanium 73	33 **As** Arsenic 75	34 **Se** Selenium 79	35 **Br** Bromine 80	36 **Kr** Krypton 84
46 **Pd** Palladium 106	47 **Ag** Silver 108	48 **Cd** Cadmium 112	49 **In** Indium 115	50 **Sn** Tin 119	51 **Sb** Antimony 122	52 **Te** Tellurium 128	53 **I** Iodine 127	54 **Xe** Xenon 131
78 **Pt** Platinum 195	79 **Au** Gold 197	80 **Hg** Mercury 201	81 **Tl** Thallium 204	82 **Pb** Lead 207	83 **Bi** Bismuth 209	84 **Po** Polonium (209)	85 **At** Astatine (210)	86 **Rn** Radon (222)
110 **Ds** Darmstadtium (281)	111 **Rg** Roentgenium (280)	112 **Cn** Copernicium (285)	113 **Uut** Ununtrium (284)	114 **Uuq** Ununquadium (289)	115 **Uup** Ununpentium (291)	116 **Uuh** Ununhexium (293)	117 **Uus** Ununseptium (295)	118 **Uuo** Ununoctium (294)

62 **Sm** Samarium 150	63 **Eu** Europium 152	64 **Gd** Gadolinium 157	65 **Tb** Terbium 159	66 **Dy** Dysprosium 163	67 **Ho** Holmium 165	68 **Er** Erbium 167	69 **Tm** Thulium 169	70 **Yb** Ytterbium 173	71 **Lu** Lutetium 175
94 **Pu** Plutonium (244)	95 **Am** Americium (243)	96 **Cm** Curium (247)	97 **Bk** Berkelium (247)	98 **Cf** Californium (251)	99 **Es** Einsteinium (252)	100 **Fm** Fermium (257)	101 **Md** Mendelevium (258)	102 **No** Nobelium (259)	103 **Lr** Lawrencium (260)

One of the chief sources of the element beryllium is a mineral known as beryl, which is made up of aluminum, silicon, and oxygen. One of its crystalline forms is aquamarine, which is cut into a sparkling pale blue gemstone. Emerald is another form of this mineral.

How the atomic structure of beryllium relates to its representation in the periodic table.

sets for each element, including, for example, electron arrangements and whether the element is normally a solid, liquid, or gas at room temperature and pressure. In many modern tables, the elements are also shaded according to type, showing which are metals, nonmetals, and metalloids. Other tables have individual shading for specific groups of elements, for example, one color for the alkali metals, one for the alkaline-earth metals, one for the halogens, and so on.

Rows are called periods

The seven main rows of the periodic table are called periods. Hydrogen and helium make up Period 1. Next come the two short periods of eight elements: Period 2 starts with lithium (atomic number 3) and ends with neon (10). Period 3 starts with sodium (11) and ends with argon (18). Then come the two long periods, each of 18 elements. Period 4 starts with potassium (19) and ends on krypton (36). Period 5 starts with rubidium (37) and ends with xenon (54). Some of the elements in the long periods 4 and 5 are called transition metals. In Period 4, the transition metals start with scandium (21) and end with zinc (30). In Period 5, the transition metals start with yttrium (39) and end with cadmium (48).

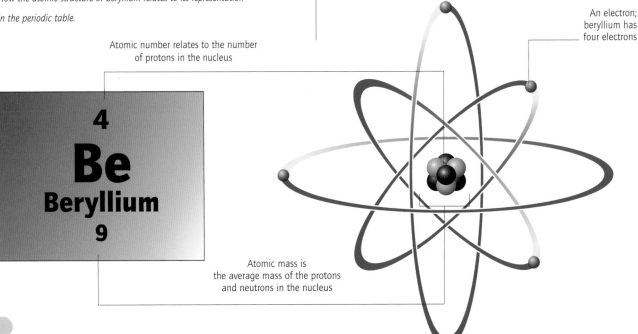

Atomic number relates to the number of protons in the nucleus

4
Be
Beryllium
9

Atomic mass is the average mass of the protons and neutrons in the nucleus

An electron; beryllium has four electrons

Period 6 is a very long row of 32 elements, starting with caesium (55) and ending with radon (86). In most modern periodic tables, Period 6 is reduced to 17 elements by moving 15 elements, called the lanthanides, to the bottom of the table. Not only does the table then fit on a normal size page, it also allows elements with similar valence to be placed in the same columns. (Valence depends on the number of electrons in the outer shell and determines the reactivity of the element.) So the transition metals in Period 6 end with mercury (80), which lies directly below cadmium, the last transition metal in Period 5.

Plants and animals rely on three of the Period 2 elements to live and grow. Carbon and the gases nitrogen and oxygen make up about 90 percent of the dry weight of all living organisms.

Period 7 is another very long period of 32 elements, which ends with the artificial element ununoctium (118). Period 7 is also shortened by moving 15 elements, called the actinides, to the bottom of the table. All of these elements are radioactive, and many have very short half-lives. Because of this, elements 93 to 118 do not occur in nature, but they have been created in laboratories by scientists.

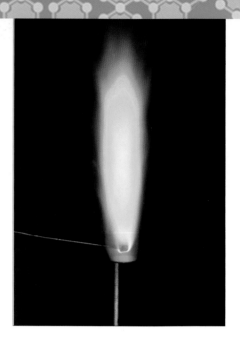

Flame tests, where a sample is burned in a flame, can be used to identify elements. On the left is copper and on the right is sodium. The distinctive strong yellow color of sodium is recognizable from streetlamps, where sodium is used in the bulb.

Columns are called groups

Elements with the same number of electrons in their outer electron shells are usually found in columns called groups. Chemists place hydrogen at the top of Group 1, but it is not really part of the group. Group 1 actually starts with lithium (3) and ends with francium (87). Unlike hydrogen, the Group 1 elements are soft, strong, metals. All of them react with water to form alkaline solutions. For this reason, the Group 1 elements are called the alkali metals.

The Group 2 elements start with beryllium (4) and end with radium (88). The Group 2 elements are known as the alkaline-earth metals. These metals also react with water to form alkaline solutions. The word *earth* comes from an old term used to describe the compounds formed when the Group 2 metals reacted with oxygen.

Groups 3 to 12 comprise the transition metals in the center of the periodic table and rare-earth metals at the bottom of the table. The chemistry of the transition metals is less predictable than that of the alkali and alkaline-earth metals. Some transition metals, such as

Period 2 of the periodic table begins with lithium and ends with neon. As the elements progress along the row, their chemical nature changes from metallic (Li and Be) and metalloid (B) to nonmetallic (C) and finally gaseous (N, O, F, and Ne).

cobalt (27) and iron (26), form many different colored compounds. Others, such as gold (79) and platinum (78), hardly react at all and can be found as pure metals in nature.

Groups 13, 14, 15, and 16 form groups of elements that do not seem as clearly related as the previous groups. Metalloids (metal-like elements), such as boron (5) and silicon (14), and many solid nonmetals, such as phosphorus (15) and sulfur (16), are found in groups 13 through 16. The halogens make up Group 17. This group starts with fluorine (9) and ends with astatine (85). All halogens are reactive, and fluorine is the most reactive of all the elements.

The Group 18 elements start with helium (2) and end with radon (86). These gases had not been discovered when Mendeleyev's original table was published in 1869. Mendeleyev added them to the

Opposite: Transition metals form compounds of many colors. That makes them very useful in the glass industry where this property helps make colored marbles.

3	4	5	6	7	8	9	10
Li	**Be**	**B**	**C**	**N**	**O**	**F**	**Ne**
Lithium	Beryllium	Boron	Carbon	Nitrogen	Oxygen	Fluorine	Neon
7	9	11	12	14	16	19	20

A HOME FOR HYDROGEN

In most versions of the periodic table, hydrogen is put above the alkali metals in Group 1 at the top left of the periodic table. There is a problem with this, however, because hydrogen is a gas and all the Group 1 elements are metals. In other versions of the table, hydrogen can be found above the halogens in Group 17. Sometimes, hydrogen appears in both groups, and sometimes it is left to float freely at the top of the table. In fact, hydrogen is a unique element that no one really knows where to place.

TRY THIS

Colors in the periodic table

Search for a few different versions of the periodic table on the Internet. Compare them to the one printed in this book. Which table do you think works best? Use a printer to make some copies of the periodic tables you have found. You could also take a photocopy of the periodic table in this book. Then shade in one color all the elements that are metals. Then shade in all the gases in another color. Shade the remaining boxes that are neither metals nor gases using a different color. You might need to do some research before you start coloring in the boxes to find out which elements are metals, which are gases, and which are neither.

RARE-EARTH METALS

In most modern versions of the periodic table, two rows of 15 elements can be found at the bottom of the table. The 15 elements in the first row are called the lanthanide elements, and those in the second row are called the actinide elements. The reason for the separation is a practical one. A period with the full complement of 32 elements is simply too long to fit on a normal page. However, most chemists agree that the chemistry of the lanthanides and actinides is similar enough for the elements to form a separate group, called the rare-earth metals.

Uranium is one of the rare-earth elements. It is sometimes added to glass to produce luminous green or yellow color when exposed to ultraviolet light.

end of his revised table in 1902. The Group 18 elements do not react with many other elements. For this reason, they are known as the noble, or inert, gases.

Numbering conventions

From the top to the bottom of the periodic table, the periods (rows) are simply numbered 1 through 7. The numbering of the groups is more problematic. There are three systems for numbering the groups. The first uses Roman numerals (I, II, III, IV, V, and so on). The second system uses a combination of Roman numerals and the letters A and B. In 1985, the International Union of Pure and Applied Chemistry (IUPAC) replaced the traditional Roman numerals and letters. The new system uses the Arabic numerals 1 to 18, starting with the alkali metals (Group 1) and ending with the noble gases (Group 18).

SCIENCE WORDS

- **Boiling point:** The temperature at which a liquid turns into a gas.
- **Melting point:** The temperature at which a solid turns into a liquid.
- **Standard conditions:** Normal room temperature and pressure.

Trends in the table

Today, the periodic table consists of 118 elements in seven periods and 18 groups. At room temperature and pressure, two of these elements are liquids (bromine and mercury), 11 are gases, and the rest are solids. Aside from hydrogen and mercury, the gases and liquids are on the right of the table. Most metals are on the left-hand side and bottom of the table. The metalloids form a diagonal line, from boron to tellurium, on the right-hand side of the table. Most nonmetals, such as carbon, oxygen, nitrogen, and the halogens, are on the right and top of the table (aside from the noble gases). Thus, there is a general trend

AN ELEMENT BY ANY OTHER NAME

Deciding what to call an element has posed a challenge to scientists throughout the centuries. Of the elements that have been known longest, most countries have their own names for elements such as gold, silver, or mercury. For example, France and Greece call nitrogen *azote*, and Germany uses *Sauerstoff* for oxygen. Some use versions of the Latin names and are very similar. Silver is *argentum* in Latin, which is changed to *argento* in Italian and *argent* in French.

To avoid confusion in international trade and ensure that scientists of all nations can talk about the same element without any risk of misidentification, element names have been standardized. The body that oversees this process is the International Union of Pure and Applied Chemistry, or IUPAC. Among its rulings are that aluminum and cesium should be known by their British spellings "aluminium" and "caesium", but that sulfur should take the U.S. spelling (not sulphur). In this set, "aluminum" is used throughout.

With new elements still being synthesized in the laboratory, IUPAC is also involved in the naming process. Often the new element has been found by two or more laboratories and they may have different ideas about what to call it. There have been many arguments over what to call the heavy elements with atomic numbers between 104 and 112. These have now been agreed as rutherfordium (104), dubnium (105), seaborgium (106), bohrium (107), hassium (108), meitnerium (109), darmstadtium (110), roentgenium (111), and copernicium (112). Elements beyond these are temporarily known by a Latinized form of their atomic number (known as a systematic element name)—ununtrium (113), ununquadium (114), and so on—until their synthesis has been confirmed and a permanent name is agreed upon.

Most of the elements are named after places or people. The places are usually where the element was first discovered or the discoverer's country. Those named after people honor famous scientists or characters from mythology.

Elements named after places

Americium—the Americas
Californium—the state of California
Darmstadtium—Darmstadt, Germany
Europium—Europe
Francium—France
Hafnium—*Hafnia*, Latin for Copenhagen
Holmium—*Holmia*, Latin for Stockholm
Lutetium—*Lutetia*, Latin for Paris
Magnesium—Magnesia, Greece
Polonium—Poland
Strontium—Strontian, Scotland
Ytterbium, Yttrium—Ytterby, Sweden

Elements named after people or gods

Bohrium—Niels Bohr
Curium—Pierre and Marie Curie
Einsteinium—Albert Einstein
Fermium—Enrico Fermi
Helium—Helios, the Greek sun god
Mendelevium—Dmitry Mendeleyev
Niobium—Niobe, a woman in Greek mythology
Nobelium—Alfred Nobel
Selenium—Selene, Greek goddess of the moon
Tellurium—*Tellus*, Latin name for Earth
Thorium—Thor, the Scandinavian god of thunder
Vanadium—Vanadis, a Scandinavian goddess

for elements to become less metal-like from left to right across a period.

The alkali metals in Group 1 are soft metals with low melting points. The alkaline-earth metals in Group 2 are harder and have higher melting points than the metals of Group 1. Moving from left to right across the periods, elements gradually get harder and have higher melting and boiling points. These properties peak at the center of the table. The hardness, melting, and boiling points then begin to fall again.

PROPERTIES OF METALS

Most elements are metals, and we see them all around us, from a paperclip to a jet aircraft. Metals also form many important compounds. These substances are used to make dyes and soaps, and even occur in our bodies.

Nearly three-quarters of all the elements on Earth are metals. Many of the most common elements are metals, and they have been used by humans for thousands of years. Today, modern technology uses metals to make everything from skyscrapers and spacecraft to medicines and paints.

People first began using metals to make tools about 5,000 years ago. Historians call that time the Bronze Age, because most metal objects were made of bronze. Bronze is a mixture of two metals: copper and tin. Bronze objects are not very strong, but they still allowed people to create a range of tools to help them survive.

From about 1900 B.C., people began using a harder metal called iron. The Iron Age had begun. Iron tools and weapons were harder and more useful than bronze ones, and civilizations that could use iron were more successful than those still using bronze. People armed with iron weapons were able to defeat fighters equipped with bronze weapons.

SCIENCE WORDS

- **Alloy:** Mixture of two or more metals or a metal and a nonmetal such as carbon.
- **Metal:** An element that is generally solid, shiny, moldable, ductile, and conductive.
- **Metalloid:** A substance with properties of both a metal and a nonmetal.
- **Ore:** A mineral that contains valuable amounts of a metal.
- **Refine:** To purify a metal by getting rid of other unwanted elements.

During the Iron Age, there were many migrations (movements of people) across Asia and Europe. As people learned to use iron, their civilizations became more powerful. As a result, they began to take over new areas of land—all thanks to a metal. Iron is still the most-used metal today. Ninety-five percent of all metal objects are made from iron.

Meet the metals

There is no strict definition of a metal, but metals tend to have many similar properties: Metals are solid in normal conditions, and most only melt and boil at high

Empty metal cans awaiting recycling. Metals are very useful substances and found in all areas of everyday life.

COLORFUL CHARACTER

Some uses of metals are obvious, like electric wires and the bolts holding cars together. Others are not so clear, like the metals contained in colored items, such as lipsticks, dyes, and paints. Many of these get their color from metals. Some metals produce many different pigments (colored substances). For example, chromium produces yellow, red, and green pigments.

The colors of many paints are produced by substances that contain metal atoms.

temperatures. They are also shiny, flexible, and ductile—they can be stretched into thin wires. Metals are also good conductors. That is, they let electricity and heat pass through them quickly.

Of the 90 elements found naturally on Earth, 65 are metals. Iron (Fe) and nickel (Ni) are the most common metals on the planet. Earth's superhot core is thought to be made of these metals. In the rocks of Earth's crust, aluminum (Al) is the most common, followed by iron, sodium (Na), potassium (K), and magnesium (Mg). Like most other metals, these elements occur as ores. An ore is a natural compound, or mineral, that contains large amounts of a metal. (A compound is a substance that is formed when the atoms of two or more elements join during a chemical reaction.) A few metals, such as gold and silver, are found pure instead of as ores.

The other metals must be refined from ore. A refined metal has been purified to get rid of other unwanted elements. Once pure, most metals are then used in alloys. An alloy is a metallic substance that is made up

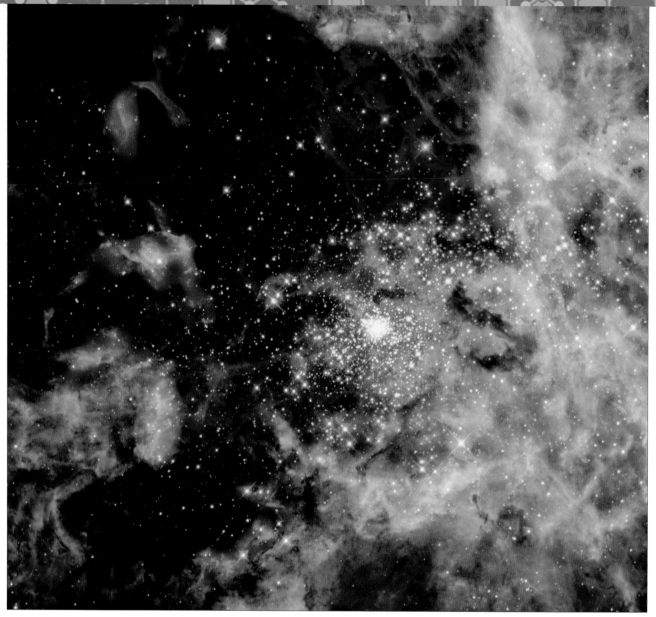

Lithium is the simplest metal. It is found in the huge clouds of gas and dust that form into stars.

of two or more metals mixed together. For example, brass is an alloy of copper and zinc.

Seven of the elements are considered metalloids. These are substances with properties of both metals and nonmetals. They are sometimes termed semimetals. Silicon (Si) is the most common metalloid. One thing that makes metalloids different is that many are semiconductors. A semiconductor only conducts

STARDUST

Scientists think that just three elements— hydrogen, helium, and lithium—were created 14 billion years ago in the first moments of the Big Bang. Hydrogen and helium gases were most abundant, but there were also tiny amounts of the metal lithium. Lithium is the lightest of all metals, and also has the smallest atom. It floats in water and oil.

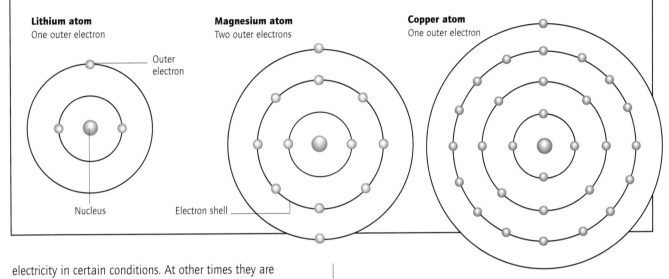

ELECTRON SHELLS

All metal atoms have only a few electrons in their outer electron shells. The atoms of a few metals have three or four outer electrons, but nearly all metal atoms have just one or two electrons. The low number of outer electrons makes metals behave and react in similar ways.

Lithium atom
One outer electron

Outer electron

Nucleus

Magnesium atom
Two outer electrons

Electron shell

Copper atom
One outer electron

electricity in certain conditions. At other times they are insulators—they block the flow of heat and energy.

Organizing the metals

Because there are so many different types of metals on Earth, chemists organize them in groups according to their atomic structure and properties. This helps chemists predict how different metals will behave when they encounter other elements.

The easiest way to learn about the different groups of metals is with a periodic table, an organized array of the elements. The periodic table provides information about individual elements and groups of elements. Metals are found on the left-hand side of the table, and nonmetals on the right. Most elements are considered metals, so they spread more than halfway across the table.

The periodic table is used to show chemical trends among the elements. The most metallic elements are located in the bottom-left corner. The most nonmetallic ones are positioned in the upper-right corner. The boundary between metals and nonmetals

is a diagonal line running through the left side of the table, from aluminum (Al) to polonium (Po).

In the periodic table, elements are formed into columns, known as groups. Each group has a number that shows where the column sits in the table.

The atoms of the members of a group have a similar structure. It is this structure that determines how an element will react and form bonds. This book examines five types of metals.

Inside metals

All elements, including the metals, are made of atoms. Atoms are the smallest pieces of an element that can retain the properties of that element.

A statue made from bronze, a mixture, or alloy, of two metals—copper and tin. Bronze objects have been made for 5,000 years, and the alloy is still a useful material today.

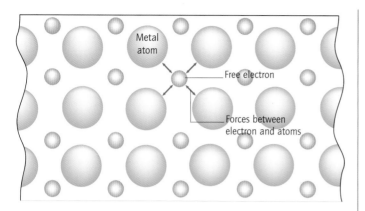

Free electrons surround metal atoms. The electrons hold the atoms together in what is known as metallic bonding.

The structure of the atom is important because it determines how that element bonds with other elements. How an element forms bonds determines many of the properties of that substance. Let us back up a little and review the inside of the atom.

At the center of the atom is the nucleus, a dense ball of positively charged particles called protons and neutral particles called neutrons.

The protons give the nucleus a positive charge. Opposite charges attract each other, while the same charges repel (push away). As a result, the nucleus attracts negatively charged particles called electrons.

SCIENCE WORDS

- **Atom:** The smallest unit of an element.
- **Bond:** An attraction between atoms.
- **Electron shell:** A layer of electrons that surrounds the nucleus of an atom.
- **Element:** The simplest type of substance made up of just one type of atom.
- **Nucleus:** The central core of an atom containing protons and neutrons.
- **Valence electrons:** The outermost electrons of an atom; they are involved in chemical reactions.

Metals share many properties, but there are also many differences between them. Mercury is perhaps the most unusual metal because it is a liquid in normal conditions.

These move around the nucleus. It is an atom's electrons that are involved in reactions.

Giving and taking

The electrons move in layers called shells that surround the nucleus. Larger atoms have more electrons than smaller ones. Their electrons are arranged in larger shells. Electrons fill the shells outward from the nucleus. The smallest shell is closest to the nucleus, while the next shell is larger and contains more electrons; each new shell is farther from the nucleus and larger.

The electrons that reside in the outermost shell (the valence electrons) are the ones involved in chemical reactions. The number of an atom's valence electrons determines how that atom bonds with other atoms.

When an atom forms a bond, it gives, takes, or shares electrons in an effort to become stable. A stable

atom is one where the outer shell is either full of electrons or empty. An atom with a nearly full outer shell will not give away its electrons easily. Instead it will gain electrons from other atoms to become stable. An atom with only a few outer electrons will give them away easily. That makes its outer shell empty and the atom stable.

Nearly all metals have atoms with just one or two valence electrons. (A handful of metals have three or four.) Therefore, metallic elements generally give away electrons to form bonds. This behavior is what makes all metals so similar.

Metallic bonds

Metals are held together by metallic bonds. These bonds form when metal atoms share their outer electrons with each other. The outer electrons break off from the atoms and form a pool, or "sea," of electrons. The sea of electrons surrounds the metal atoms. Each free electron is attracted to the several nuclei around it.

GOLD AND GREED

The Inca people lived in the Andes Mountains of Peru from 1438 to 1533. They constructed great cities of stone buildings in the mountains. Inca buildings are all the more amazing because they were built without metal tools. Incas could not purify copper or iron. Instead they used hard stones to make hammers, axes, and other equipment. However, Inca civilization used large amounts of another metal—gold. Inca people dug up pure gold, which they called the "sweat of the Sun." They used it to make cups, jewelry, and statues, but gold is too soft to make other tools. Gold was so common that it was not very valuable to the Incas. However, the first Europeans to come to Peru had different values.

Spanish explorers were the first to visit the Incas in 1532. The Incas presented their visitors with fine cloth, but the Spanish leader, Francisco Pizarro (c. 1475-1541), was more interested in their gold. After beating him in battle, Pizarro held Atahualpa, the Inca king, as a prisoner until his people paid a huge ransom. The Incas filled one room with gold and two more with silver items, but Pizarro did not keep his side of the bargain and executed Atahualpa anyway.

Gold Inca mask. Gold is mined in its pure form from the ground. It is more commonly found in some regions than in others.

Because the particles are being pulled in all directions at once, the sea of electrons forms a "glue" that holds the metal atoms together.

The sea of electrons can flow through the metal. This ability gives metals many of their physical properties, such as conductivity.

Properties of metals

As we have seen, metallic elements share similar atomic structures and they bond to each other in a certain way. As a result metals share many properties:

• **Solid and shiny:** Tightly packed metal atoms form a solid and are able to reflect light well, making the metal appear shiny.

• **Flexible:** The sea of electrons that binds metal atoms can flow around. The atoms are not held firmly in one place, so metals can be bent or hammered into a new shape without breaking.

It takes a lot of heat energy to melt solid metal into a liquid. When it is molten, it can be poured into a mold. When the metal cools down, it will be hard and very tough.

• **Ductile:** As a metal is stretched into a wire, the sea of electrons continues to flow around the atoms. As a result the metallic bonds can hold even thin wires together.

• **Conductive:** The sea of electrons is constantly moving. If the electrons are made to flow in one direction, they form an electric current.

• **High melting and boiling points:** Metallic bonds are strong bonds, so solid metals are generally tough solids. Strong metallic bonds also require a lot of heat energy to break them so the solid can melt into a liquid, and even more to boil a liquid metal into a gas.

Reactions of metals

Metals are reactive elements because they readily give or share their valence (outer) electrons. Two common chemical reactions involving metals are combination and displacement reactions.

During these reactions, metal atoms become ions. An ion is an atom that has lost or gained one or more electrons. Metal atoms lose their outer electrons and form positively charged ions. Atoms that gain electrons from metals during a reaction become negatively charged ions.

Ions with opposite charges are attracted to each other. This attraction creates a bond between the ions

Metals are highly versatile. These pylons are made from steel, which makes them very strong structures. The steel is sometimes coated with a layer of zinc, another metal, to prevent it from rusting. The electricity wires strung between the towers are made of aluminum. This metal is a good conductor, but is also very light.

REACTIVITY SERIES

Metals can be organized into a reactivity series—a list with the most reactive metals at the top and least reactive at the bottom. The reactivity of metals is determined by how easily their atoms lose their outer electron or electrons. The list below shows the reactivity of some familiar metals.

Potassium	K	
Sodium	Na	React with water
Calcium	Ca	
Magnesium	Mg	
Aluminum	Al	
Zinc	Zn	
Iron	Fe	React with acid
Tin	Sn	
Copper	Cu	
Mercury	Hg	
Silver	Ag	
Gold	Au	Unreactive
Platinum	Pt	

and forms an ionic compound. These compounds normally form when a metal gives one or more of its electrons to a nonmetal.

A common example of an ionic compound is potassium chloride (KCl). It is created in a combination reaction, when potassium (K) bonds with chlorine (Cl). With one valence electron to give away, potassium reacts easily. Chlorine is a nonmetal gas. Its atoms need one electron to become stable. If potassium and chlorine are put together, the potassium atoms will lose their outer electrons and give them to the chlorine:

$$2K + Cl_2 \rightarrow 2KCl$$

Reactivity

Some metals are more reactive than others. A reactive metal loses its outer electrons more easily than a less reactive one. As a result, metal atoms are often involved in displacement reactions. These occur when a reactive element replaces a less reactive element in a compound. For example, potassium is more reactive than calcium (Ca), so pure potassium will react with calcium chloride ($CaCl_2$) to produce pure calcium and potassium chloride. However, pure calcium is not reactive enough to displace potassium from its compounds.

ALKALI METALS

Alkali metals are the most reactive group of metals. The most common alkali metals are sodium and potassium. These metals are included in many useful compounds, such as table salt, baking powder, borax, and gunpowder.

The elements in Group 1, the first column on the left of the periodic table, are known as the alkali metals. The group includes six metals—lithium (Li), sodium (Na), potassium (K), rubidium (Rb), caesium (Cs), and francium (Fr). The first five of these metals were discovered in the 19th century when scientists worked out how to purify them from compounds found in nature. Potassium and sodium were discovered by English chemist Humphry Davy (1778-1829) in 1807. Lithium was discovered by Swede Johan Arfwedson (1792-1841) in 1817. German Robert Bunsen (1811-1899) discovered caesium and rubidium in 1861. Francium was discovered in 1939, but it is the second rarest element on Earth and very little is known about it. (The rarest element is astatine; At.)

Although each chemist used a different method to discover the elements, they realized the new metals had a similar atomic structure and shared many chemical

Soap compounds contain the alkali metals sodium and potassium. The compounds form bubbles when mixed with water.

and physical properties. For example, the alkali metals, known as such because many of their compounds are alkalis, are much softer than most other metals.

Atomic structure

The alkali metals have only one valence electron in the outermost shell. As a result, they readily give away this electron to become more stable. Hydrogen also has

SCIENCE WORDS

- **Alkali:** A compound that contains large amounts of hydroxide (OH^-) ions.
- **Chemical reaction:** A process in which atoms of different elements join or break apart.
- **Compound:** A substance formed when atoms of two or more different elements bond together.
- **Ion:** An atom that has lost or gained one or more electrons.

one electron to give away and is sometimes included in Group 1. However, hydrogen is a gas in normal conditions and is not considered to be a metal.

It is their single outer electron that makes the alkali metals very reactive. A reactive element forms bonds with other atoms easily during chemical reactions.

Alkalis and acids

Alkali metals are so called because they form compounds that are alkaline. Alkalis are also referred to as bases. They are ionic compounds—made up of ions with opposite charges that are attracted to each other. Alkalis contain high numbers of negative hydroxide ions (OH^-). An alkali's positive ion is generally a metal. For example, sodium hydroxide (NaOH) is made of a sodium ion (Na^+) bonded to a hydroxide ion.

An acid is the opposite of an alkali. It has a high number of hydrogen ions (H^+). When an alkali reacts with an acid, the hydroxide and hydrogen ions combine to produce water (H_2O). The other elements in the acid and alkali compounds also form a product, which chemists call a salt. For example, sodium hydroxide and hydrochloric acid (HCl) react to form water and sodium chloride (NaCl). Sodium chloride is table salt, which is used to flavor food. This reaction is written like this:

NaOH + HCl → NaCl + H_2O

Chemists test the pH of a substance using universal indicator paper. This paper changes color with pH. Alkalis make the paper turn blue. Acids make the paper red. Neutral compounds make the paper green.

Chemists measure the number of ions in acids and alkalis using the pH scale. The pH scale runs from 0 to 14. A pH lower than 7 is considered acidic, and a pH higher than 7 is considered alkaline. Water has a pH of 7 so it is neutral—neither acid nor base.

Properties

Because all of the alkali metals have a similar atomic structure, they also look alike and behave in the same

ALKALI-METAL COMPOUNDS

Compound	Formula	Common name	Use
Sodium chloride	(NaCl)	Table salt	Used to flavor food
Sodium bicarbonate	($NaHCO_3$)	Baking powder	Helps baked foods rise
Sodium hydroxide	(NaOH)	Lye	Used to make soap
Potassium carbonate	(K_2CO_3)	Potash	Used to make glass, enamel, and soap
Potassium chloride	(KCl)	–	Used as a plant fertilizer
Potassium nitrate	(KNO_3)	An ingredient of saltpeter	Used to make gunpowder and glass and to cure meat

way. Alkali metals have the following physical and chemical properties:

• **Soft:** All the alkali metals are soft enough to be cut with a steel knife. As the size and mass of an alkali-metal atom goes up, the metal gets softer. So the farther down the column on the periodic table, the softer the metal. For example, caesium is almost liquid at room temperature. The softness is due to weak metallic bonds. Alkali-metal atoms have just one

---

PURIFYING ALKALI METALS

The alkali metals are very reactive. Although many of them are common in nature, they always occur combined with other elements to make compounds, such as table salt.

Chemists cannot extract alkali metals using chemical reactions and have to use electricity instead. An electric current separates the elements in certain compounds through a process called electrolysis. Even the most reactive elements, including alkali metals, can be separated in this way. However, more reactive elements require larger electric currents.

During electrolysis, positively and negatively charged rods are immersed in a liquid containing the compound to be split apart. Each rod attracts particles with an opposite charge, breaking the compound's bonds and separating the different ingredients.

This was the technique used by Humphry Davy (1778–1829) in 1807 to purify first potassium and then sodium. That was the first time anyone had purified alkali metals. Davy used a simple battery called a pile to produce an electric current. Davy's assistant was Michael Faraday (1791–1867), who continued the study of electricity and later invented the electric motor.

SCIENCE WORDS

- **Electron shell:** A layer of electrons that surrounds the nucleus of an atom.
- **Ionic bond:** A bond produced when oppositely charged ions are attracted to each other.
- **Molecule:** Two or more atoms connected together.
- **Salt:** A compound made from positive and negative ions that forms when an alkali reacts with an acid.

---

electron each to form the sea of electrons, so electrons are spread thinly among the atoms. As a result, the bonds that hold the atoms together are not strong.

• **Shiny:** All the alkali metals are shiny. Most are silvery gray, although caesium has a golden tinge.

• **Good conductors:** All the alkali metals conduct heat and electricity well.

• **Distinctive colors:** When the alkali metals are burned, they produce flames with characteristic colors. Lithium burns dark red, sodium is yellow, potassium is lilac, rubidium is also red, and caesium produces a blue flame.

• **Highly reactive:** The alkali metals are stored in oil so they do not react with oxygen in the air. Some reactions are so fast and intense that they create an explosion of heat and gas. Alkali metals with large atoms are more reactive than the metals with small and light ones—large atoms lose their single outer electrons more easily during reactions.

Bond formation

The single outer electron of the alkali metals is the key to how their atoms behave with other elements. To become stable, an alkali-metal atom must lose its single outer electron to empty its outer shell. It does this by forming an ionic compound.

An ionic compound is produced when a metal atom gives an electron to a nonmetal atom. The atom that gives away an electron loses a negative charge and becomes a positive ion. Chemists call positively charged ions cations. The atom that takes an electron receives an extra negative charge and becomes a negatively charged ion. Chemists call that an anion. The opposite charges of the cation and anion attract each other, which results in an ionic bond forming between them, creating a compound.

Sodium chloride is created in this way from sodium (Na) and chlorine (Cl). Sodium is a typical alkali metal. It has one electron to give away before becoming stable. Chlorine is a nonmetal gas in need of one electron to fill its outer shell and become stable. If you put sodium and chlorine in a container together, sodium will lose its electron (becoming the cation Na^+) while chlorine takes the same electron (becoming the anion Cl^-). The Na^+ cation bonds with the Cl^- to form the compound NaCl, the chemical formula for table salt. The reaction is written as:

$$2Na + Cl_2 \rightarrow 2NaCl$$

Forming alkalis

One of the most important reactions of alkali metals is with water. This is the reaction that produces the main alkali compounds for which the metals are named. In most cases, the reaction is violent, with the metal bursting into flames. Caesium reacts so explosively that it will shatter even a thick glass container.

REACTIVITY

Alkali metals with large atoms are more reactive than those with smaller atoms. In a smaller atom such as lithium, the outer electron is nearer to the nucleus. As a result, the electron is held in place more strongly and is less likely to be involved in a chemical reaction. In a larger atom, such as potassium, the outer electron is held in place weakly and is more easily lost during a reaction.

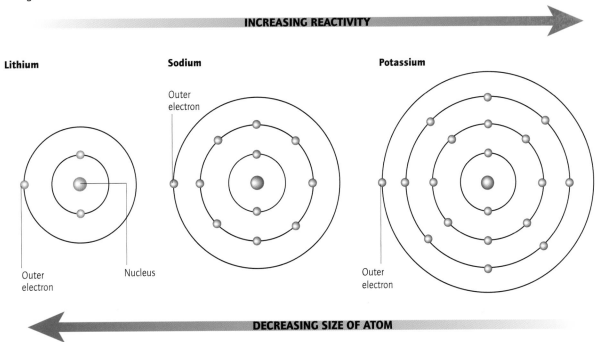

INCREASING REACTIVITY →

Lithium

Sodium

Outer electron

Potassium

Outer electron   Nucleus

Outer electron

← **DECREASING SIZE OF ATOM**

TRY THIS

Fizzing rocket

The reactivity of alkali metals can be used to power a homemade rocket. You will need a toilet-paper roll, an empty film canister, a paper plate, some water, and half an indigestion tablet, such as Alka-Seltzer.

Tape the toilet-paper roll so it stands upright on the plate. Half fill the canister with water. Put the plate on the ground in an open space outside. Drop the half tablet into the canister and quickly close the lid, making sure it is on tight. Turn the canister upside down and drop it into the toilet-paper roll. Stand back and wait for several seconds. Caution: do not look down the toilet-paper roll.

Soon the canister will launch into the air. The water will spill out into the toilet-paper-roll launcher and plate, so you may need to replace them if you want to repeat the activity several times.

The canister rocket is powered by the reaction between the tablet and the water. The tablet contains sodium bicarbonate, which produces bubbles of carbon dioxide gas when it reacts with water. The gas builds up inside the canister. Eventually the pressure of the gas gets so high that it pushes off the canister's lid so it can escape. As the gas rushes out, it pushes the canister up through the launcher and high into the air.

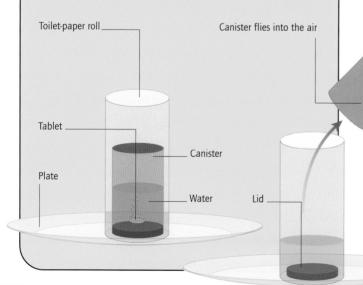

Toilet-paper roll

Canister flies into the air

Tablet

Plate

Canister

Water

Lid

The yellow light of these streetlights is produced by sodium gas. The gas gives out light when an electric current runs through it.

As the least reactive alkali metal, lithium reacts with water more slowly. When you add lithium (Li) to water (H_2O), the metal atom combines with an oxygen and hydrogen atom from the water. Together they become a lithium cation (Li+) and a hydroxide anion (OH^-). These ions bond forming the alkali lithium hydroxide (LiOH). The hydrogen atoms left over from the water form into pairs (H_2). These hydrogen molecules are released as gas. The equation for this reaction is:

$$2Li + 2H_2O \rightarrow 2LiOH + H_2$$

Sources

Sodium and potassium are the two most important alkali metals; they are the sixth and seventh most abundant elements on the planet. Sodium and potassium salts are dissolved in seawater. Sodium makes up more than 1 percent of seawater. Potassium is less common.

Compounds of both metals are found in many types of minerals and rocks. The other alkali metals are quite rare. Francium is radioactive so its atoms break apart into other elements. None of the alkali metals are found as pure elements in nature because they are so reactive. Instead, they occur as salts. A salt is a compound formed when an acid reacts with an alkali.

PURIFYING ALKALI METALS

Sodium carbonate is manufactured using the Solvay process. Calcium carbonate ($CaCO_3$) is dissolved in brine (1), which is also saturated with ammonia, NH_3 (2). Carbon dioxide (CO_2) is bubbled through the mixture in a reaction tower (3), resulting in sodium bicarbonate, $NaHCO_3$ (4), or baking soda. This is then heated (5) producing sodium carbonate (Na_2CO_3) and carbon dioxide.

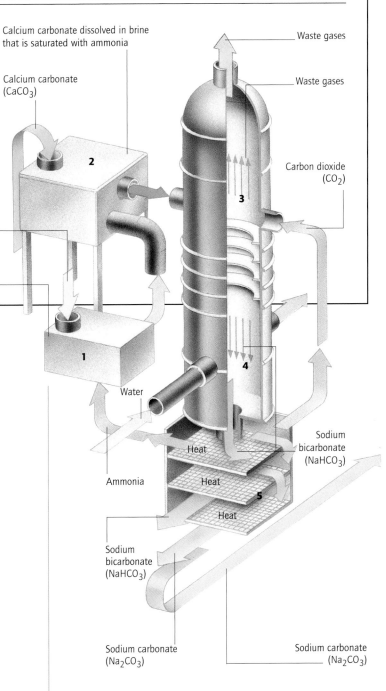

Calcium carbonate dissolved in brine that is saturated with ammonia

Calcium carbonate ($CaCO_3$)

Waste gases

Waste gases

Carbon dioxide (CO_2)

Brine (sodium chloride, NaCl, dissolved in water)

Brine saturated with ammonia

Water

Ammonia

Sodium bicarbonate ($NaHCO_3$)

Heat

Heat

Heat

Sodium bicarbonate ($NaHCO_3$)

Sodium carbonate (Na_2CO_3)

Sodium carbonate (Na_2CO_3)

Sodium's most common salt is sodium chloride (table salt). Others include saltpeter (sodium nitrate; $NaNO_3$), which is an ingredient of gunpowder and used to make glass, and borax (sodium borate; $Na_2B_4O_7$), which was once used in soaps.

Potassium chloride (KCl) is that metal's most common salt. Another one is potash (potassium carbonate; K_2CO_3). This is also called salt of tartar. Potash is used to make soft, luxury soaps.

In most cases, the alkali metals are purified by electrolysis, a process that breaks salts apart using electricity. The equation for this process looks like this:

$$2NaCl \rightarrow 2Na + Cl_2$$

Uses

The number of industrial uses for the alkali metals is huge. For example, the yellow streetlights you see along major roadways get their color from sodium gas glowing inside. Sodium bicarbonate ($NaHCO_3$), or baking powder, is used to make cakes. The compound reacts with water in the cake mix and releases carbon dioxide gas (CO_2). This gas is trapped as bubbles inside the cake, making it light and spongy.

Alloys of the alkali metals are also very useful. Sodium is used to purify titanium and mercury, while an alloy of sodium and potassium collects the heat produced in nuclear reactors.

The alkaline-earth metals are similar to the alkali metals, but are harder and less reactive. This group's most familiar member is calcium. Calcium-containing compounds, such as limestone, occur in large amounts in nature.

The elements in the second column of the periodic table, called Group 2, are known as the alkaline-earth metals. These six elements—beryllium (Be), magnesium (Mg), calcium (Ca), strontium (Sr), barium (Ba), and radium (Ra)—were not purified until the 19th century. However, many of their compounds had been known about since much earlier times. For example calcium-containing compounds, such as marble, a type of calcium carbonate ($CaCO_3$), has been used as a building material for thousands of years. As early as the first century B.C., the Romans were making buildings from concrete that contained quicklime (calcium oxide; CaO).

Alkaline-earth metals are named for these and other compounds. Earth is an old name for a naturally occurring compound. Before the study of chemicals became scientific in the 17th century, people thought different earths were elements themselves. They noticed that some of the earths were similar to the alkaline substances such as lye (sodium hydroxide; NaOH). They were called alkaline earths. Once it was found that these substances were really compounds containing metals, the metals were named the alkaline-earth metals.

Seashells are made of calcium carbonate, a compound that contains an alkaline-earth metal.

SCIENCE WORDS

- **Compound:** Substance formed when atoms of two or more different elements bond together.
- **Nucleus:** Central core of an atom.
- **Radioactive:** When an atom has an unstable nucleus that breaks apart.

Calcium and magnesium, the two most common alkaline-earth metals were discovered by English chemist Humphry Davy (1778–1829). He made this discovery in 1807, a year after isolating some of the first alkali metals.

The last member of the group to be discovered was radium, which was isolated by Marie (1867–1934) and Pierre Curie (1859–1906) in 1898. In 1911, Marie Curie

won the Nobel Prize in Chemistry for this important discovery. Radium is radioactive, so particles break away from its atoms' nuclei. This changes the number of particles in the atom, so it becomes an atom of another element. The particles given out by radioactive elements are termed radiation.

Atomic Structure

The atoms of alkaline-earth metals have two electrons in their outer shell. These are the valence electrons, which take part in chemical reactions.

To become stable, the atoms must give away or share these two electrons. In most cases, the alkaline-earth metals readily give away the two electrons, making them reactive metals.

Properties

The alkaline-earth metals all have two valence electrons and so have similar properties. Their properties resemble those of the alkali metals, but their behavior is less extreme. Alkaline-earth metals have the following properties:

• **Soft:** They are harder than the alkali metals, but still softer and more malleable (flexible) than most other metals.

• **Good conductors:** All of them conduct heat and electricity well.

ALKALINE-EARTH METAL COMPOUNDS

Compound	Formula	Common name	Use
Calcium oxide	CaO	Quicklime	Used in building materials
Calcium carbonate	$CaCO_3$	Limestone, calcite	Used in mortar and toothpaste
Calcium sulfate	$CaSO_4$	Gypsum	A fertilizer and fireproofing agent
Magnesium carbonate	$MgCO_3$	Magnesite	Gymnastic chalk
Magnesium hydroxide	$Mg(OH)_2$	Milk of magnesia	Indigestion remedy
Magnesium silicate	$MgSi_4O_{10}$	Soapstone	Talcum powder
Magnesium sulfate	$MgSO_4$	Epsom salts	Laxative

• **Distinctive colors:** All these metals burn with bright white flames, but when heated they produce light with a certain color. For example, calcium produces light of a dark red color, strontium a brighter red, and barium green.

• **Reactive:** Alkaline-earth metals are very reactive, but less so than alkali metals. The alkaline-earth metals hold onto their two outer electrons more tightly than the alkali metals hold onto their one outer electron. The metals become more reactive going down the group.

HARD WATER

Water that contains the alkaline-earth metals calcium or magnesium is commonly called hard water. The alkaline-earth metals dissolved in hard water react with soap and stop it from forming bubbles.

Hard water comes from deep underground, where it trickles through rocks containing calcium and magnesium compounds.

Removing the metals "softens" the water. Hard water also tastes different from soft water because it contains more minerals.

Hard water produces limescale when it is heated. This chalky substance blocks pipes and coats heating elements in kettles. Softening the water removes the scale.

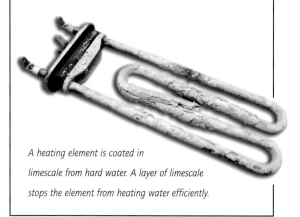

A heating element is coated in limescale from hard water. A layer of limescale stops the element from heating water efficiently.

A strip of magnesium burns with a very bright white flame. Magnesium is used in emergency flares because it burns so brightly.

• **Shiny:** Pure alkaline-earth metals are silver colored and shiny. However, the more reactive members of the group, such as strontium and barium, soon become dull gray. That is because the metals react with oxygen in the air and are covered in a layer of metal oxide.

Sources

Calcium and magnesium are the two most common alkaline-earth metals. Calcium makes up about 3 percent of the Earth's rocks and magnesium makes up about 2 percent. The other alkaline-earth metals are rare. None of the alkaline-earth metals are found as pure elements in nature because they are so reactive.

TRY THIS

Hard and soft water

Both rainwater and distilled water are much like what people call "soft water." These liquids contain few ions, atoms that have gained or lost electrons. Epsom salt is magnesium sulfate ($MgSO_4$). When it dissolves in water, the resulting solution is like "hard water."

1 Fill two glasses about half full of rainwater or distilled water. Fill the third glass about half full of tap water.

2 Add about 1 spoonful of Epsom salts to one of the glasses containing rainwater or distilled water.

3 Add three drops of dish-washing soap to each glass.

4 Stir the water in each glass rapidly. Observe the results.

The glass with only distilled water or rainwater should be quite foamy and the glass containing magnesium sulfate should have little foam. How does your tap water compare?

The glass on the left contains distilled water, which is soft. Notice the bubbles on the surface. The middle glass contains distilled water with Epsom salts added, making the water hard. Thus, the dish-washing soap does not bubble. The glass on the right is tap water. There are some bubbles on the surface but not many, so the water from this particular region must be a little hard.

Calcium occurs mostly in soils as calcium carbonate, an ingredient in limestone. Magnesite, or magnesium carbonate ($MgCO_3$), is one of the most common natural magnesium compounds.

Alkaline-earth metals are purified by electrolysis. This is a process in which a powerful electric current is used to split a compound into its elements. Calcium chloride ($CaCl_2$) is used for this process. As well as pure metal, the reaction also produces chlorine gas (Cl_2):

$$CaCl_2 \rightarrow Ca + Cl_2$$

Bond formation

Most alkaline-earth metal compounds are ionic. Ionic compounds are formed when one atom loses electrons and another gains them. An alkaline-earth metal atom forms an ion by losing its two outer electrons. This results in an ion with a charge of 2+, which is written as, for example, Ca^{2+}. The lost electrons are picked up by the atoms of another element. Those atoms become negatively charged ions. Ions with opposite charges are attracted to each other and they bond into a compound.

TRY THIS

Testing alkalis and acids

Alkaline-earth metals make compounds that are alkaline. You can investigate how they react with an acid using this activity. You will need lemon juice, some milk of magnesia (an indigestion medicine), and indicator paper. Lemon juice is an acid, which contains many positive hydrogen ions. It turns indicator paper red. Milk of magnesia is magnesium hydroxide, $Mg(OH)_2$, an alkali. It contains many negative hydroxide ions and turns indicator paper blue.

Begin by testing the juice with a piece of indicator paper. Put the paper on one side to dry so you can compare its color with later tests. Add three tablespoons of milk of magnesia to the juice and stir the mixture. Re-test the liquid with a strip of indicator paper. Compare the color of this strip. It should be less red than the first. This is because the milk of magnesia and some of the acid ions have reacted to produce neutral products.

Keep adding more magnesia and re-testing the mixture. The mixture will gradually lose its acidity and become alkaline. At this point the paper will turn dark green.

Lemon juice is acidic, but as more and more milk of magnesia is added to the lemon juice, the mixture becomes increasingly alkaline. Testing with indicator paper shows a gradual change from red to dark green.

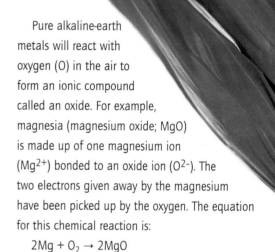

Pure alkaline-earth metals will react with oxygen (O) in the air to form an ionic compound called an oxide. For example, magnesia (magnesium oxide; MgO) is made up of one magnesium ion (Mg^{2+}) bonded to an oxide ion (O^{2-}). The two electrons given away by the magnesium have been picked up by the oxygen. The equation for this chemical reaction is:

$$2Mg + O_2 \rightarrow 2MgO$$

Chemical reactions

Calcium carbonate ($CaCO_3$) from limestone has many uses. For example, it is used in the production of steel. However, it is also turned into a quicklime (CaO) through a simple reaction. When limestone is heated, it decomposes into quicklime and carbon dioxide gas (CO_2):

$$CaCO_3 \rightarrow CaO + CO_2$$

Quicklime is a reactive substance. It is an ingredient in plaster, mortar, and cement. When water (H_2O) is added to quicklime, a reaction takes place that is known as slaking. The reaction produces slaked lime or calcium hydroxide—$Ca(OH)_2$:

$$CaO + H_2O \rightarrow Ca(OH)_2$$

SCIENCE WORDS

- **Acid:** A compound that contains large amounts of hydrogen (H^+) ions.
- **Alkali:** A compound that contains large amounts of hydroxide (OH^-) ions.
- **Atom:** The smallest piece of an element that retains the properties of the element.
- **Bond:** An attraction between atoms.
- **Ion:** An atom that has lost or gained one or more electrons.

A gymnast swings on a bar. He has a powder on his hands to help him grip. The powder is magnesium carbonate. It is often called "chalk," but it is not the same as the substance used on chalkboards in schools.

Slaked lime is an alkali—a substance that contains a lot of hydroxide ions (OH^-). Alkalis react with acids, which are compounds that contain a lot of hydrogen ions (H^+).

When quicklime is added to mortar or another building material it is mixed with water. The two compounds react, and the resulting slaked lime then undergoes another reaction. Carbon dioxide in the air dissolves in water inside the mortar to make a carbonic acid (H_2CO_3). This acid reacts with the slaked lime to form calcium carbonate and water. The reaction looks likes this:

$$Ca(OH)_2 + H_2CO_3 \rightarrow CaCO_3 + 2H_2O$$

Calcium carbonate occurs naturally in limestone, and following these reactions the mortar has literally turned to stone.

Uses

Alkaline-earth metals have many other uses. For, example, magnesium is alloyed with aluminum to make strong but light objects, such as aircraft. Beryllium is added to copper to make it harder.

Until about 1950, radium was used to make paints that glowed in the dark. The glow came from the radioactive atoms releasing radiation. We now know that radiation of this kind can be harmful to humans. Today radium is only used in safe ways.

WRITING ON THE WALL

Teachers use a common calcium compound in the classroom. The chalk used to write on chalkboards is a type of limestone, which contains calcium carbonate. Chalk forms from the remains of tiny sea organisms. When they die, their shells, which contain calcium carbonate, build up in piles in shallow waters. Over the years the shells form a thick layer and are squeezed into chalk.

Aluminum, the most abundant metal in Earth's rocks, belongs to Group 3 of the periodic table. This group's other members are much rarer.

The elements in the 13th column of the periodic table, called Group 3, include the metals aluminum (Al), gallium (Ga), indium (In), and thallium (Tl). Aluminum is the most important and most abundant metal in this group. The group also includes boron, which is a metalloid.

Aluminum-containing compounds were used by the ancient Greeks and Chinese. Roman doctors also used them to slow bleeding from cuts. They called the compounds alums, and that is where we get the name aluminum from. The metal was first purified in 1825 by Danish chemist Hans Christian Oersted (1777–1851).

Gallium, indium, and thallium were all discovered in the mid-19th century using spectroscopes, instruments that read the unique light pattern produced when materials are heated.

SCIENCE WORDS

- **Covalent bond:** A bond in which atoms share electrons.
- **Ionic bond:** A bond produced when oppositely charged ions are attracted to each other.
- **Malleable:** Describes a material that can be bent easily or pounded into a flat sheet.
- **Metalloid:** A substance with the properties of both a metal and a nonmetal.
- **Molecule:** Two or more atoms connected together.
- **Ore:** A mineral that contains valuable amounts of a metal.
- **Refine:** To purify a metal by removing unwanted elements.

Atomic structure

All Group 3 metals have three valence electrons in their outer electron shells. To become stable, atoms must give or share these three electrons. Losing three electrons requires a lot more energy than losing just one or two. As a result the Group 3 metals are only mildly reactive, much less so than alkali metals, for example.

Properties

Aluminum, gallium, indium, and thallium have many of the classic metal properties. They are all shiny, and either gray or silver in color. They also conduct heat

Crushed aluminum cans waiting to be recycled. This metal is recycled because pure aluminum is very expensive to make.

and electricity very well. However, it is their soft and flexible nature that makes these metals unusual.

Aluminum is the second most malleable (moldable) metal on Earth (second only to gold). Gallium, indium, and thallium are very soft. Each has an unusually low melting point and they are nearly liquids in normal conditions.

Sources

Aluminum is the most abundant metal in the Earth's crust, making up about 7 percent of rocks and minerals. Yet it is one of the most difficult metals on the planet to make in a pure form.

Like most metals, aluminum does not appear in nature as a free element. The main aluminum ore is alumina (aluminum oxide; Al_2O_3). Pure alumina is a colorless and extremely stable compound that takes a lot of energy to split into individual elements. The compound is known also as corundum. It is the main substance in ruby and sapphire gemstones.

Aluminum has only been produced in large amounts for about 100 years. It is purified through a complex process that involves both electrolysis and smelting. Today, many aluminum objects are made from recycled metal. It takes 20 times less energy to reuse aluminum than it does to purify it.

Gallium, indium, and thallium are rare and found mostly in the ores of other metals, such as copper, zinc, and lead. They are extracted as by-products when these other metals are refined.

GROUP 3 COMPOUNDS

Compound	Formula	Common name	Use
Aluminum chlorohydrate	$Al_2(OH)_5Cl$	—	Used in deodorants
Aluminum oxide	Al_2O_3	Alumina; corundum	Found in rubies and sapphires
Gallium arsenide	GaAs	—	Produces laser light
Indium phosphide	InP	—	Used in semiconductors
Thallium bromide	TlBr	—	Used in heat detectors
Thallium sulfate	Tl_2SO_4	—	Rat and ant poison

Bond formation

The three valence electrons in the outer shells of Group 3 metals are key to how they react with other elements. To become stable, an atom of one of these metals must give away its three electrons to empty its shell.

Most metals bond ionically, but the Group 3 elements can also form covalent bonds. An ionic bond is one that forms when ions with opposite charges attract each other. The atoms of Group 3 metals form ions by losing three outer electrons to become, for example, Al^{3+}. These ions are attracted to negatively charged ions, which have gained electrons.

A covalent bond forms when atoms share pairs of electrons instead of giving away or gaining them. By sharing, each atom can fill its outer shell with electrons and become more stable. A few Group 3 compounds, such as aluminum iodide (AlI_3), are covalent. However, most Group 3 metals form ionic compounds.

Alumina (Al_2O_3) is a typical example of an ionic compound. It forms when aluminum comes in contact with the oxygen (O_2) in the air. The equation for the chemical reaction is:

$$4Al + 3O_2 \rightarrow 2Al_2O_3$$

In each molecule of alumina, two Al^{3+} ions are bonded to three O^{2-} ions.

Large passenger aircraft, such as this Boeing 747, are made from aluminum alloys. Aluminum is strong but also very light, making large aircraft light enough to fly.

Gallium's melting point is 86°F (30°C). The heat from a hand is enough to turn gallium into a liquid.

Alumina forms as a thin layer on the surface of the metal. That stops oxygen from getting to the pure metal underneath so the reaction cannot continue.

Gallium, indium, and thallium are all more reactive than aluminum. As the metal with the largest atoms, thallium is the most reactive. It must be stored in water to prevent it from reacting with oxygen in the air.

Chemical reactions

Aluminum is often used as a reducing agent. A reducing agent is a compound that gives away electrons during a chemical reaction. Aluminum is the reducing agent for an important reaction called the thermite process. This reaction is used to make pure iron from iron oxide (Fe_2O_3). The aluminum atoms give electrons to the iron ions (Fe^{3+}) during the reaction. As a result, the aluminum atoms become ions (Al^{3+}) and bond to the oxide ion (O^{2-}) to form alumina. The Fe^{3+} ions become atoms of pure iron. The reaction looks like this:

$$Fe_2O_3 + 2Al \rightarrow Al_2O_3 + 2Fe$$

Common chemical reactions of gallium, indium, and thallium are harder to describe, partly because they are rare. Gallium can corrode other metals—a chemical reaction in which one metal oxidizes another.

Uses

Aluminum is one of the most useful metals on Earth. No other metal has been as important since iron replaced bronze as the most useful metal at the dawn of the Iron Age. Although iron is still the most-used metal, aluminum's properties make it useful in different ways. For example, it is light and so is used to make aircraft and electricity cables that are hung from pylons. It is also malleable and can be molded into many shapes. Perhaps the most common shape is that of an aluminum can.

Most aluminum products are alloys (mixtures of other elements, usually other metals). Small amounts of copper, zinc, magnesium, and silicon are added to it to make it harder. Alumina is used to protect steel (an iron alloy) from rusting. A thin layer of the compound is coated on the steel. The coating stops oxygen and moisture from getting to the iron underneath.

Charles Martin Hall

Charles Martin Hall (1863-1914) was a U.S. chemist who invented an inexpensive way of making pure aluminum. Hall made his discovery in 1886 aged just 23. He did his research in a laboratory in his house in Oberlin, Ohio.

The process became known as the Hall-Héroult process because Frenchman Paul Héroult (1863-1914) developed a similar system at the same time. Before the Hall-Héroult process was invented, pure aluminum was as expensive as silver. Although aluminum compounds were common, it was very difficult to refine the metal.

Hall's discovery changed all that and made it possible for aluminum to be used in all kinds of ways. The Hall-Héroult process is still used today. It involves electrolysis, in which an electric current splits alumina (aluminum oxide; Al_2O_3) into pure aluminum and oxygen. This is done at a high temperature so the alumina is melted into a liquid.

TIN AND LEAD

Tin and lead are familiar metals because they have been used by people for many thousands of years. Both are easy to purify and are unreactive and so are often used to protect other metals from damage.

The metals tin (Sn) and lead (Pb) appear in the 14th column of the periodic table, which is known as Group 14. Tin and lead are the only metals in this group. The other Group 14 elements are germanium and silicon, which are classed as metalloids, and carbon, which is a nonmetal.

People have used tin and lead for 7,000 years. Tin was added to copper to make the alloy bronze. Lead was bent into tubes (which could be used for transporting water) and other useful shapes.

No one knows who first discovered and named these metals. Their chemical symbols come from their Latin names—*stannum* for tin, and *plumbum* for lead.

It is easy to make pure tin and lead. Rocks sometimes contain pure lead. However, neither of the metals is very common in nature.

Atomic structure

The atoms of tin and lead each have four valence electrons in their outer shell. To become stable, these atoms need either eight or no electrons in their outer shells. That can be achieved by losing four electrons

Model soldiers made of an alloy of tin and lead. The alloy is easy to melt and pour into molds.

or gaining four. Both options require a lot of energy. As a result, tin and lead are not very reactive elements, and they are not involved in many chemical reactions with other elements.

SCIENCE WORDS

- **Alloy:** Mixture of two or more metals or a metal and a nonmetal such as carbon.
- **Electron shell:** A layer of electrons that surrounds the nucleus of an atom.
- **Valence electrons:** The outermost electrons of an atom, which are involved in chemical reactions.

COMPOUNDS AND ALLOYS OF TIN AND LEAD

Compound	Formula	Common name	Use
Lead acetate	$Pb(C_2H_3O_2)_2$	Sugar of lead	A poisonous, sugarlike substance used in dyes and varnish
Lead carbonate	$(PbCO_3)_2 \cdot Pb(OH)_2$	White lead	A white pigment (coloring)
Lead oxide	PbO	Litharge	Once used to make yellow paint and glass
Lead tetraoxide	Pb_3O_4	Red lead	A red pigment
Niobium-tin	Nb_3Sn	–	A superconductor that conducts electricity very well
Bronze	60% Cu, 40% Sn	–	An alloy containing tin (Sn) and copper (Cu)
Pewter	85% Sn, 15% Pb	–	A substitute for silver once used to make shiny objects
Solder	60% Sn, 40% Pb	–	An alloy used to fuse metals
Tin tetrachloride	$SnCl_4$	Stannic chloride	Used to toughen glass

A microchip is soldered into place. The solder is an alloy of tin and lead. It is melted by a hot soldering iron. The melted alloy flows around the chip. The solder cools and becomes solid again, holding the chip in place.

While the four valence electrons make tin and lead fairly unreactive, they also enable the atoms to form very stable bonds. A stable bond is one that is not easily broken. Once a tin or lead atom bonds with another element, that bond is very hard to break.

Tin and lead are described as "poor metals" because they do not react in the same way as other metals. The only metals that are less reactive than tin and lead are the so-called precious metals, such as gold and platinum.

Properties

The atomic structure of tin and lead helps create an important characteristic of both elements—the ability to resist corrosion. Corrosion is a chemical reaction between a metal and its environment, usually the oxygen and water in the air, which weakens the metal. Rusting is a type of corrosion.

Tin and lead do not rust because they react only slowly with oxygen to form oxides. Like other lead and tin compounds, the oxides are very stable. They form a thin layer on the surface of the metals. This layer acts as a barrier between the air and the metal, which prevents any more reactions from taking place.

Tin and lead also share other properties. Both are soft metals that can be bent or molded easily. They have low melting and boiling points compared to other metals. Both are also poor conductors of electricity and heat compared to other metals.

Sources

Both tin and lead occur only in very small quantities in the Earth's crust. If you took a random scoop of one million pieces, or parts, of the Earth's crust, only two parts would be tin and twelve parts would be lead. Scientists call this way of measuring parts per million, or ppm. In this case, the Earth's crust is 2 ppm tin and 12 ppm lead.

Galena is the most common lead-containing compound in nature.

Tin occurs as ores—minerals that contain a useful amount of the metal. Much of the world's tin is contained in the mineral cassiterite, which is mainly tin oxide (SnO_2). Cassiterite tends to be located in soft ground close to the surface. As a result, it is mined using the open-pit method. Some mines have tunnels leading down to the ore. However, an open-pit mine is just a huge hole dug into the ground. The largest tin mines are in Malaysia.

Lead is sometimes found as a pure metal, especially near volcanoes where the heat causes minerals to react. Most lead is found in the form of the mineral galena (lead sulfide; PbS). Galena and other lead ores are generally located deep underground in hard rocks. The metal is also found in the ores of other metals, such as silver and copper.

Gasoline used to have lead compounds in it to help it burn evenly. However, the lead came out in the exhaust fumes and damaged people's health. Today, most gasoline is unleaded.

Chemical reactions

Having four valence electrons makes tin and lead unreactive metals. To form a bond with another atom, the tin or lead atom must give away its four outer electrons and become an ion. Tin and lead atoms form ions with a charge of 4+. Losing four electrons requires a lot of energy, which is why they do not react easily.

Ions are attracted to other ions with an opposite charge. These ionic bonds create an ionic compound. For example, tin ions (Sn^{4+}) bond to two oxide ions (O^{2-}) to form cassiterite (SnO_2). Galena (PbS) is one lead ion (Pb^{4+}) bonded to one sulfide ion (S^{4-}).

Pure tin and lead are removed from their compounds by reacting them with carbon (C). This is a displacement reaction in which the carbon takes the place of the metal in the compound. The reaction requires heat, which is supplied by burning the carbon. (Coal is a fuel made of mainly carbon.) For example, tin is extracted from cassiterite, in a chemical reaction that looks like this:

$$SnO_2 + 2C \rightarrow 2CO + Sn$$

Uses

Tin and lead have many uses. Tin is used to protect other metals from rusting. Food cans are coated with a layer of tin for this reason. They are still referred to as tin cans in some parts of the world, although most of the metal in them is steel (a strong alloy of iron containing carbon and other elements).

Tin is also a common ingredient in alloys. Bronze, pewter, and solder all contain large proportions of tin. Pewter and solder also contain lead.

Lead is used a lot less than tin because it is poisonous. It used to be used widely and made people ill. Today, it is used in safe ways, to make brass, ammunition, glass, ceramics, and cable covers. As a very heavy metal, lead is used in weights. More than half of the lead used today comes from recycled products.

SCIENCE WORDS

- **Compound:** A substance formed when atoms of two or more different elements bond together.
- **Conductor:** A substance that carries electricity and heat well.
- **Ion:** An atom that has lost or gained an electron or electrons.
- **Mineral:** A naturally occurring compound, such as those that make up rocks and soil.
- **Ore:** A mineral that contains valuable amounts of a metal.

TRANSITION METALS

Nearly half of all metals are transition elements. These metals form a block across the center of the periodic table. Many of the most common and familiar metals, such as copper, iron, and gold, are transition metals.

The elements between the third and twelfth columns of the periodic table are called the transition series. All of these elements are metals.

The transition metals include some metals that have been known about for thousands of years, such as iron (Fe), silver (Ag), and copper (Cu). The other metals in the series have been discovered over the past 300 years. Transition metals with lower atomic numbers, and therefore with smaller and lighter atoms, were generally discovered before the elements with larger, heavy atoms. Heavy metals tend to be more reactive than lighter ones, and thus are more difficult to isolate from compounds.

Widely used transition metals include manganese (Mn), chromium (Cr), cobalt (Co), nickel (Ni), tungsten (W), and titanium (Ti). The rarer transition metals include molybdenum (Mo), palladium (Pd), rhodium (Rh), and zirconium (Zr).

SCIENCE WORDS

- **Alloy:** Mixture of two or more metals or a metal and a nonmetal such as carbon.
- **Electron shell:** A layer of electrons that surrounds the nucleus of an atom.
- **Metal:** A substance that is solid, shiny, moldable, and that can carry electricity.
- **Ore:** A naturally occurring substance that contains valuable amounts of a metal.
- **Valence electron:** One of the outer electrons in an atom that is involved in chemical reactions.

Atomic structure

The transition metals form a series rather than a group. That is because they all share an unusual atomic structure that separates them from all other metals. However, they also have a varying number of outer electrons, so they cannot be formed into a group in the same way as other metals. Nevertheless, like most of the other groups of metals, transition metals have just one or two electrons in their outermost electron shells. These electrons are valence electrons and so are involved in chemical reactions with other elements.

With one or two outer electrons, transition elements react in the same way as alkali metals and alkaline-earth metals. The transition metals are generally less reactive than these other groups. We find the reason for this by looking more closely at the elements' atomic structures. As well as in the outer electron shell, transition elements also have valence electrons in the next shell in toward the nucleus.

Layers of electron

An atom's electrons are arranged in shells that fit inside one another. The smallest and innermost shell contains just two electrons. The second shell is larger and can hold up to eight electrons. The third shell is larger still and has room for up to 18 electrons. However, instead of filling up with this number of electrons, once the third shell has eight electrons, it stops accepting any more. The fourth shell then begins to fill up. Once the fourth shell has two electrons, the third shell begins to accept electrons again.

Adding electrons

To illustrate this, let us compare the atomic structures of calcium and scandium. Calcium is the last element in the periodic table before the transition series begins. Scandium is the first member of the series. Calcium atoms have four shells. The third shell has eight electrons, and the fourth has two. Scandium atoms also have four shells. As in calcium, the fourth shell has two electrons, but the third shell has nine.

The third shell continues to fill up, producing a series of metal atoms with four electron shells. Most of these atoms have two outer electrons, although a few such as chromium and copper have one.

The third shell is finally full in the atoms of zinc, where it contains 18 electrons. At this point the fourth and outer shell begins to fill up again.

Many gemstones are colored by transition metals. Chromium makes emeralds green and rubies red, while titanium makes sapphires blue.

Following zinc, atoms of the metal gallium form. Gallium is not a transition metal. Its atoms have a third shell with 18 electrons, and a fourth shell with three electrons.

The fourth shell continues to gain electrons until it holds eight in the atoms of the gas krypton. As happened with the third shell, the fourth shell now stops accepting any more electrons. A fifth electron shell begins to form. Once this shell holds two electrons, the fourth shell beneath it then continues to fill. Another series of metal atoms with five shells and one or two outer electrons is formed. The same process also occurs in atoms with six shells. The transition series ends with mercury (Hg).

Properties

Transition metals tend to be good conductors and they are the toughest metals, with much higher melting

TRANSITION-METAL COMPOUNDS

Compound	Formula	Common name	Use
Brass	67% Cu, 33% Zn	–	Alloy used to make ornaments and musical instruments
Cobalt oxide	CoO	Cobalt blue	A deep blue compound used to color glass and china
Copper sulfate	$CuSO_4$	–	Used as a pesticide
Hematite	Fe_2O_3	Black diamond	The main iron ore
Lead chromate	$PbCrO_4$	Chrome yellow	A bright yellow pigment
Manganese dioxide	MnO_2	Pyrolusite	Used in batteries
Stainless steel	90% Fe, 10% Cr	–	Used to make shiny objects that do not rust
Vanadium pentoxide	V_2O_5	–	A catalyst used to produce sulfuric acid

Many Sun-protection creams contain zinc oxide, a white substance that blocks ultraviolet light. Ultraviolet (UV) light is invisible radiation that is produced by the Sun. UV radiation can damage the skin, causing sunburn and tanning. Zinc oxide is also used to make space suits UV-proof.

TRY THIS

Rusting nails

Iron objects rust when exposed to oxygen. Rust is actually an iron oxide that forms on the surface of iron objects when exposed to air. In this activity, you will explore how sealing the nail against oxygen prevents rust from forming.

You will need three glasses, a galvanized nail and two ungalvanized nails. Place one nail in each glass. You may need to polish the ungalvanized nails with sandpaper. Do not polish the galvanized nail. Pour water into one of the glasses containing an ungalvanized nail and into the glass containing the galvanized nail. Dip the last nail in a little vegetable oil and pour water over it. Add enough vegetable oil to completely cover the surface of the glass. Leave the glasses for several days and then observe.

The galvanized nail has not rusted because it is protected with a rust-resistant coating. The nail covered with oil has not rusted because the oil provides a protective coating, preventing oxygen getting to the nail.

From left to right, the photographs show a galvanized nail, an ungalvanized nail, and an ungalvanized nail coated with oil and covered with water. Only the ungalvanized nail has rusted since the galvanized nail has a protective coating and the oil prevents oxygen reaching the other nail.

points than the metals in other groups. However, there are some notable exceptions. For example, mercury is liquid at room temperature, and gold is very malleable.

Many of the elements' properties are the result of how their atoms bond together. In most cases, the transition metals have a lot of valence electrons. As well as being involved in reactions, these also help form metallic bonds. The more electrons metal atoms use to form these bonds, the stronger they will be. Having strong bonds between its atoms makes a metal very hard. The strong bonds hold each atom in a fixed position, and it takes a large force to break them apart or push them into a different shape. However, many hard transition metals, such as iron and chromium, are also brittle. That is, when they do break they shatter into pieces. These metals are made less brittle by being alloyed with other substances.

The strong bonds also make the metal atoms pack tightly together, and as a result some transition metals are very dense. Measuring a substance's density is a

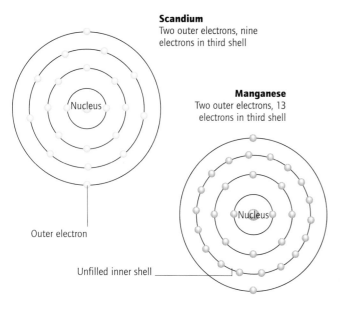

Scandium
Two outer electrons, nine electrons in third shell

Nucleus

Outer electron

Manganese
Two outer electrons, 13 electrons in third shell

Nucleus

Unfilled inner shell

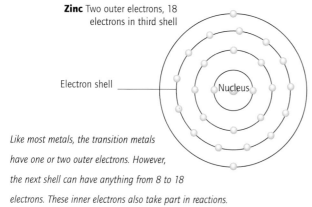

Zinc Two outer electrons, 18 electrons in third shell

Electron shell

Nucleus

Like most metals, the transition metals have one or two outer electrons. However, the next shell can have anything from 8 to 18 electrons. These inner electrons also take part in reactions.

A bridge made of steel, an alloy of iron and carbon with other metals mixed in. Steel is extremely strong, but can also be molded and bent.

SCIENCE WORDS

- **Compound:** Atoms of different elements bonded together.
- **Conductor:** A substance that carries electricity and heat well.
- **Density:** A measure of how tightly atoms are packed into a solid.
- **Malleable:** When a material can be bent easily or pounded into a flat sheet.
- **Metallic bond:** A bond between a group of metal atoms that are sharing a pool of electrons.

way of comparing how big it is (volume) with how heavy it is (weight). A handful of a dense substance weighs more than the same volume of a less dense substance. The densest element of all is the transition metal osmium (Os). A cube of this metal with sides measuring 1 inch (2.5 cm) weighs a surprising 13 ounces (370 g), that is 22.5 times heavier than the same volume of water.

The strong bonds also result in high melting and boiling points because it takes a lot of energy to break

Steel nails are coated with zinc, in a process called galvanization, to prevent them from rusting when they are exposed to air.

the bonds. Most transition metals melt at temperatures above 1832°F (1000°C). Tungsten has the highest melting point of any metal: 6192°F (3422°C).

Sources

A few transition metals, such as mercury, gold, and platinum, are found pure in nature. Others occur in minerals combined with other elements. Useful metals, such as iron and copper, are extracted from such minerals, which are called ores. Ores are minerals that contain large amounts of a valuable metal. Other transition metals are rare and are not refined from their own ores. Instead, they are usually produced as by-products during the production process of other more common metals.

Iron is the planet's most common element. Scientists think that the Earth's core is a huge ball of hot iron and nickel (another transition metal). However, only about 5 percent of the Earth's crust is iron, making it the fourth most abundant element in rocks. Most iron occurs bonded to oxygen to make compounds called iron oxides.

The other transition metals that are mined for their ores are nickel, zinc, and titanium. Of these transition metals, titanium is the ninth most abundant and zinc is the 23rd most abundant element in the Earth's crust. Nickel and copper are not far behind.

The ores are generally found near the surface, so they are dug up directly from the surface, creating huge holes or pits in the process.

The ores of iron and other transition metals are refined to make pure metals using a process called smelting. In this process, metal oxides are reacted with carbon (C). During the reaction, the carbon takes oxygen out of the ore, leaving pure metal behind.

Rarer transition metals are purified in the same way, generally as by-products. For example, rhodium is a by-product of nickel production, and cadmium is a by-product of zinc refining.

Valence electrons

The atomic structure of transition metals has a great effect on how these elements form bonds with other elements. Atoms bond to each other by giving, taking, or sharing their valence electrons. The atoms do this to fill or empty their outer electron shells.

MEASURING TEMPERATURE

We take advantage of mercury being a liquid at everyday temperatures in a tool used to measure temperature: the thermometer. This instrument was invented in 1592. It is a hollow glass tube marked with the temperature and filled with mercury. As it gets warm, the mercury expands and moves up the glass tube, indicating a change in temperature. Today, mercury thermometers are only used under controlled conditions because the metal is extremely poisonous.

Mercury used to be used in clinical thermometers, designed to measure body temperature, but these are rare today.

The transition metals have valence electrons in two electron shells rather than just the outer one like most other elements. Because of this, the way their atoms use these electrons to form bonds with other atoms is far more complicated.

Most of the nontransition elements must lose, gain, or share a fixed number of electrons in order to become stable and form a bond. However, transition metals can form compounds by using a varying number of their valence electrons. That makes the chemical behavior of transition metals quite complex. In many cases, an atom of a transition metal can form three or four different compounds with atoms of another element.

Oxidation states

Chemists work out how a transition element forms its bonds by calculating something called the oxidation state. Despite its name, the oxidation state is just a number that tells chemists how many electrons an atom has lost or gained as it formed a compound with other elements. For example, when the nontransition metal magnesium (Mg) reacts with the nonmetal oxygen (O_2), it loses its two valence electrons. As a result it forms an ion with a charge of 2+ (Mg^{2+}). An ion is an atom that has lost or gained an electron and so has become charged. The oxygen gains two electrons to fill its outer shell and forms the negatively charged ion O^{2-}. In this example, magnesium has an oxidation state of +2, while oxygen has a state of –2.

Most transition metals can have more than one oxidation state. For example, those of manganese are +7, +4, +3, and +2. In other words, manganese atoms can lose up to seven electrons during a reaction. That is more than any other metal. Iron has oxidation states of +3 and +2, while copper's are +2 and +1.

A few transition metals have just one oxidation state. For example, scandium's is +3, and zinc only forms ions with a oxidation state of +2.

Forming bonds

The oxidation state of a transition metal tells chemists how many ions are needed to make a compound. Like

A vast pit created by digging copper ore from the ground.

most other metals, transition metals make ionic compounds. These are produced when ions bond together. Ions are attracted to other ions with an opposite charge. This attraction is what creates a bond between the two ions.

While the ions that make up a compound are charged, the compound itself is neutral—it does not have a charge. That is because the opposite charges of the ions balance each other. So the oxidation state, or charge, of a transition-metal ion determines how many ions it bonds with.

For example, when copper has an oxidation state of +1 (Cu^+), it takes two ions to form a compound with an oxygen ion (O^{2-}). The compound has the formula Cu_2O. Chemists call this compound cuprous oxide, or copper (I) oxide—the "I" is "one" in Roman numerals. When copper has an oxidation state of +2 (Cu^{2+}) it forms cupric oxide—copper (II) oxide (CuO).

Helping reactions

The transition metals are often good catalysts. A catalyst is something that makes a chemical reaction go faster. One example, known as the Haber process, uses iron (Fe) to make ammonia (NH_3). The chemical reaction looks like this:

$$N_2 + 3H_2 \xrightarrow{Fe} 2NH_3$$

Putting its symbol above the arrow shows that the iron is the catalyst and not a reactant or product. The

iron plays a part in the reaction, but is not used up by it. In this example, the iron catalyst gives and takes electrons (changing its oxidation state), so the nitrogen (N) and hydrogen (H) atoms have more chances to bond with each other.

Another reason transition metals are good catalysts is because other substances can stick to their surfaces. While the substances are stuck, atoms can rearrange to form new chemical substances. One chemical reaction that uses a transition-metal catalyst in this way converts small organic (carbon-based) chain molecules

METALS IN THE BLOOD

Iron is vital in blood because it bonds with oxygen. The iron is part of a large molecule called hemoglobin. This molecule makes our blood red. Hemoglobin picks up oxygen molecules that are breathed into the lungs and then carries them throughout the body. However, not all animals use iron for this purpose. The king crab, which is an ocean-living relative of scorpions and spiders, uses copper compounds instead of iron ones to transport oxygen around in its body. Because of this, the crab's blood is blue instead of red.

A magnified image of blood cells traveling through a blood vessel. The cells are red because they contain a lot of hemoglobin.

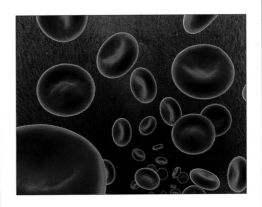

TRY THIS

Iron in food

Many foods have iron added to them to make them healthier. You can extract the iron from breakfast cereal. You will need some cereal flakes, a Ziploc bag, a cup of water, plastic food wrap, a paper towel, and a small magnet taped to a wooden stick. Seal some flakes in the bag and crush them into a fine powder. Pour the powder into a bowl and mix it with the water. Stir the mixture of cereal for 10 minutes with the magnet covered in plastic food wrap. Wipe the food wrap with a paper towel. You should see tiny specks of black powder on the towel—the iron in your cereal. Repeat with other cereals and compare the amount of iron you find.

into larger ones. For example, ethane (C_2H_4) reacts with hydrogen (H_2) to become propane (C_3H_6) when heated in the presence of a nickel catalyst.

A metal catalyst that works in this way adsorbs the other atoms. Notice that this word does not have the same meaning as absorb. When something is absorbed it becomes mixed into another substance. When it is adsorbed, a substance clings to the surface of another, but remains separate.

Different uses

Transition metals are the metals used in industry to make everything from rust-proof roofs to earrings.

However, many of the metals are also important for the chemical reactions that take place inside living bodies. Without tiny amounts of several transition metals in their bodies, people would become ill.

As we have seen (box on page 51), an iron compound is used in our blood to transport oxygen. It also makes blood red. Human bodies use other transition metals in similar ways. Several are ingredients of vitamins. Cobalt, for example, is a vital part of vitamin B_{12}, which occurs naturally in meat, eggs, and dairy products. The body also needs minute amounts of chromium, manganese, copper, zinc, and several other transition elements to stay healthy. However, if people eat large amounts of these metals they will become ill.

In industry, iron is the most important of all metals. It is easy to find and inexpensive to refine. About 95 percent of all the pure metal produced is iron. In its pure form, iron is brittle and not very useful. However, when it is alloyed with a small amount of carbon it becomes a flexible and strong alloy called steel.

Many of the other transition metals are rarely used in their pure form. Instead, they are mixed with iron to make steels with different properties. For example, chromium is added to make stainless steel, which does not rust. Steel containing molybdenum is very hard. Steel with a coating of zinc is called galvanized steel. This alloy is also rust-proof and is often used outdoors.

There are four types of cobalt ions, each one with a certain oxidation state. The oxidation number goes up each time the cobalt loses an electron.

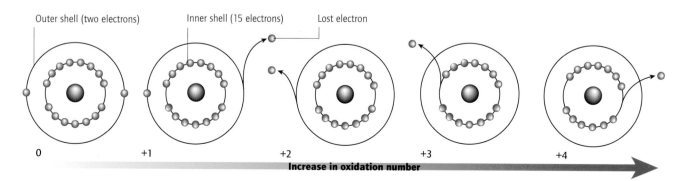

Outer shell (two electrons)   Inner shell (15 electrons)   Lost electron

0   +1   +2   +3   +4

Increase in oxidation number

Molten (liquid) iron is poured from a giant ladle into molds.

Transition metals that are used on their own include gold, silver, and titanium, which is both stronger and lighter than steel. Copper is a good conductor and is used to make electric wires. Zinc, cadmium, and nickel are used in batteries.

Magnetism

Three transition metals—iron, cobalt, and nickel—can be made into magnets. A magnet is an object that has two poles, known as north and south. When two magnets come together, the like poles repel each other, while opposite poles attract. The magnetic force that does this is produced by the electrons spinning inside the atoms of these three metals. No other elements, metal or nonmetal, can be used to make magnets.

PURIFYING METALS

Many metals are purified from their ores by a process called smelting. Iron is the main metal to be smelted, but manganese, cobalt, and nickel are also purified in this way.

Smelting is a series of chemical reactions in which the ore reacts with carbon (C) and then carbon monoxide (CO). The products of the reactions are pure metal, carbon dioxide (CO_2), and waste, known as slag. The reaction's chemical equation looks like this:

$$2Fe_2O_3 + 3C = 4Fe + 3CO_2$$

Evidence of iron smelting dates back thousands of years but no one knows who discovered the technique. Today, iron smelting takes place in a chimney-shaped blast furnace. Iron ore is heated with coke, a type of coal that is almost pure carbon. The ore melts and reacts with the carbon to produce carbon monoxide. This gas also reacts and removes the last of the oxygen from the ore to produce pure molten (melted) iron and carbon dioxide. Oxygen is also blasted through the mixture to burn away impurities.

SCIENCE WORDS

- **Catalyst:** An element or compound that helps a chemical reaction occur more quickly, but that is not altered by the reaction.
- **Ion:** An atom that has lost or gained one or more electrons.
- **Ionic bond:** A bond produced between oppositely charged ions.
- **Oxidation state:** A number used to describe how many electrons an atom has lost or gained.

METALLOIDS

The metalloids are the most unusual of all elements. They have properties of both metals and nonmetals. Many metalloids are semiconductors, which are substances used in electronics, such as computers and cell phones.

The metalloids, also known as the semimetals, are elements that have both metal and nonmetal properties. These six elements—boron (B), silicon (Si), germanium (Ge), arsenic (As), antimony (Sb), and tellurium (Te)—form a jagged diagonal line separating the metals on the left hand side of the periodic table from the nonmetals on the far right hand side. Polonium (Po), a radioactive element, is also sometimes considered a metalloid.

Arsenic and antimony have been used for thousands of years. Arsenic was commonly used as a poison and to make glass. Ancient Egyptians used poisonous antimony compounds in eye makeup. The other metalloids were discovered from the late 18th through the 19th century.

The metalloids blend metallic and nonmetallic properties. Some are hard and slightly shiny; others are crumbly powders. A few conduct electric currents while others block them. In addition, unlike metals, metalloids are brittle and shatter easily.

SCIENCE WORDS

- **Metal:** A hard but flexible element. Metals are good conductors. Their atoms have only a few outer electrons.
- **Metalloid:** An element that has both metallic and nonmetallic properties.
- **Nonmetal:** An element that is not a metal or metalloid. Nonmetals are poor conductors. Their atoms tend to have several outer electrons.

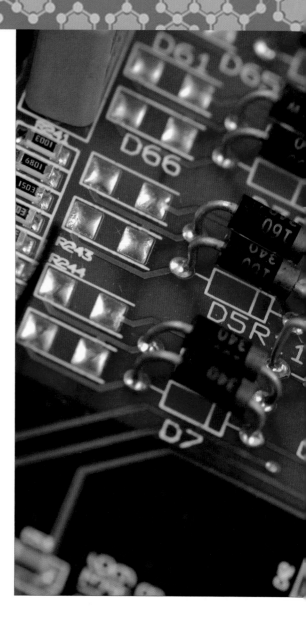

A circuit board with microchips and other electronics that contain metalloids, such as silicon and arsenic.

Atomic structure

The metalloids belong to several groups in the periodic table—from column 13 to column 16. As a result, metalloids have a variety of atomic structures.

Boron has three electrons in its outermost shell; silicon and germanium have four outer electrons; arsenic and antimony have five outer electrons; tellurium and polonium have six valence electrons. These different atomic structures influence the properties of the metalloids considerably.

Properties

As a result of their varying atomic structures, there are no properties shared by all metalloids. Instead some metalloids are more metallic than others, while some are more nonmetallic. For example, pure germanium and polonium look more like metals than other metalloids, while boron and arsenic are more nonmetallic. Most metalloids exist in two forms when pure—one metallic, the other nonmetallic.

Sources

Silicon is perhaps the most important metalloid. It is the second most abundant element in the Earth's crust, making up more than a quarter of the Earth's rocks.

Silicon is never found uncombined in nature. Its most common compound is with oxygen—silicon dioxide (SiO_4). This substance is commonly called silica and it is perhaps most familiar as the tiny crystals that make up sand. Quartz is also a form of silica that is found in many rocks, such as granite. Flint is another form of the compound found in rocks. Many precious stones are colored forms of silica, including jasper, opal, agate, and onyx.

Although silicon compounds are very easy to find, the other metalloids are not. They almost always occur bound to other elements. In many cases, metalloids are produced as by-products when refining other metals.

METALLOID COMPOUNDS

Compound	Formula	Common name	Use
Antimony trioxide	Sb_2O_3	–	A fireproofing agent
Silicon dioxide	SiO_2	Silica or sand	Used to make glass and concrete
Sodium borate	$Na_2B_4O_7$	Borax	A component of soaps, cleaners, and bleach
Sodium silicate	Na_4SiO_5	Silica gel	A drying agent
Gallium arsenide	GaAs	–	Used in solar cells and lasers
Germanium tetrahydride	GeH_4	Germane	Used to make semiconductors
Cadmium zinc telluride	CdZnTe	–	An alloy used in radiation detectors and to make holograms
Lead arsenate	$PbHAsO_4$	–	An insecticide

A crystal of quartz, which is a natural form of silica. Quartz is one of the most common minerals found in rocks. Sand is made up of tiny grains of quartz.

Arsenic commonly occurs as arsenopyrite (FeAsS), a compound of iron (Fe), arsenic (As), and sulfur (S). Because arsenic is poisonous and has few uses, it is not usually extracted from this ore. Instead, arsenic is a by-product in the treatment of other metals.

Boron has two main sources, the minerals borax and kernite. Both are forms of sodium borate ($Na_2B_4O_7$). The largest deposits of these minerals are underneath Boron, California, a town named for the metalloid.

PROPERTIES OF METALLOIDS

Metalloid	Appearance	Conductivity
Boron	Metallic and nonmetallic forms	Insulator
Silicon	Metallic and nonmetallic forms	Semiconductor
Germanium	Metallic	Semiconductor
Arsenic	Metallic and nonmetallic forms	Semiconductor
Antimony	Metallic	Semiconductor
Tellurium	Nonmetallic	Insulator
Polonium	Metallic	Insulator

Minerals containing the other metalloids do not exist in large amounts. Antimony occurs as a sulfide mineral called stibnite (SbS_3). However, antimony is more easily made as a by-product of silver and lead production. Tellurium is a common impurity in gold, lead, and copper. Germanium is a by-product of refining these metals and also zinc. Radioactive polonium is produced when radium breaks down.

Bond formation

All the metalloids except boron have four or more valence electrons in their outermost shell. Because they need eight electrons to become stable, the metalloids most often get the extra outer electrons to fill their shells by sharing them with other atoms. This sharing forms covalent bonds.

Silica (SiO_2), the most common metalloid-containing compound, is held together by covalent bonds. The reaction that produces silica looks like this:

$$Si + O_2 \rightarrow SiO_2$$

However, the way atoms bond to form silica is more complicated than this equation shows. An oxygen atom has to share two electrons with other atoms to become stable. A silicon atom has four electrons to share. In silica, each oxygen atom gets its two electrons from two silicon atoms and is bonded to both of them. Although its formula is SiO_2, each silicon atom is bonded to four oxygens. Silica's bonds connect all the atoms in a vast network, or lattice. That makes it a very hard and stable compound.

Uses

The most important modern use of metalloids is in semiconductors. The main semiconducting metalloids are silicon and germanium. Other metalloids, such as arsenic, are added to semiconductors in tiny amounts to adjust their properties. This process is called doping.

Semiconductors are substances that conduct electricity in the presence of energy such as heat, light, or electrical energy. For example, thermistors are semiconductors influenced by heat. They are used in thermometers and thermostats. Light-sensitive semiconductors are used in solar cells, which generate electricity from sunlight, and photoreceptors, which detect light. Digital cameras take pictures by recording the image formed on photoreceptors behind the lens.

Computers and similar machines are controlled by semiconductors that are influenced by electric currents. These devices act as switches and mechanisms that work together in large numbers to carry out complex tasks.

A thin wafer of silicon with electronic components etched on its surface. The wafer will be cut up into chips.

SCIENCE WORDS

- **Conductor:** A substance that carries electricity and heat well.
- **Covalent bond:** A bond in which two or more atoms share electrons.
- **Electricity:** A stream of charged particles moving through a substance.
- **Insulator:** A substance that does not carry an electric current or heat.
- **Semiconductor:** A substance that conducts only in certain conditions.

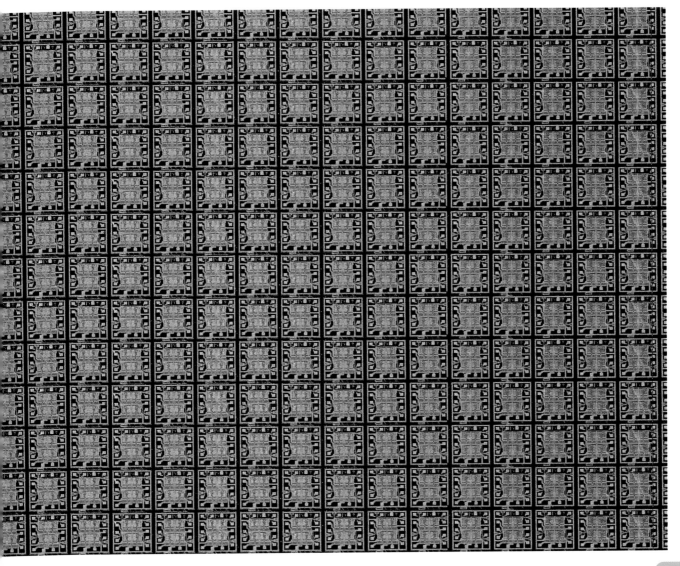

LANTHANIDES AND ACTINIDES

The rare-earth metals form two rows of elements below the main body of the periodic table. The first row contains the lanthanides (lanthanum to lutetium). The second row contains the actinides (actinium to lawrencium).

Look at the periodic table on pages 8–9 of this book. Follow the elements along Period 6. The period starts with caesium (55), then barium (56). The atomic number then jumps to hafnium (72) and continues in sequence until radon (86) at the end of the row. The same thing happens in Period 7. After radium (88), the atomic number jumps to rutherfordium (104).

The missing elements lanthanum (57) to lutetium (71) and actinium (89) to lawrencium (103) appear in two separate rows at the bottom of the periodic table. The elements in the first row are called the lanthanide elements. The elements in the second row are called the actinide elements. Together, these elements are called the rare-earth metals.

SCIENCE WORDS

- **Alloy:** Mixture of two or more metals or a metal and a nonmetal such as carbon.
- **Boiling point:** The temperature at which a liquid turns into a gas.
- **Melting point:** The temperature at which a solid turns into a liquid.
- **Ore:** Mineral that contains useful elements such as aluminium or copper.
- **Radioactivity:** The release of energy that results when the nucleus of an atom breaks down.
- **Transuranium elements:** Elements with an atomic number greater than that of uranium, which is 92.

Physical properties

The rare earths share many common properties. For this reason, it is often difficult to tell them apart. All are silvery white to gray solids with shiny surfaces, but they tarnish (discolor) in the air. The discoloration occurs because the metals readily react with oxygen in the air. The oxygen combines with the metal to form a compound called a metal oxide. The thin layer of metal oxide coats the surface of the metal. Like most metals, the rare earths are good conductors of heat and electricity.

In nature, many rare-earth metals occur mixed with other elements to form rocks and minerals. Minerals that contain valuable elements are called ores. Because the rare earths are all so similar in their chemical properties, they often occur together and are difficult to separate. Monazite is an ore of several

Uranium extraction is generally carried out in open-pit mines, which reduces exposure of miners to the poisonous radioactive gases that can accumulate in underground mines.

mixed rare-earth metals and the elements phosphorus and oxygen. The rare-earth metals are often found in combination with nonmetals. Each metal atom gives up three electrons in its outer electron shell to form chemical bonds with the nonmetal atom. In some cases, the atom may lose just two or four outer electrons, forming separate compounds with different properties.

The lanthanide elements

The name rare-earth metal is slightly misleading for the lanthanide elements. The lanthanides are not as rare as chemists first thought. Some lanthanides are more common than better-known metals such as platinum or lead, for example. Only promethium has to be made artificially.

The lanthanides are relatively soft metals, but their hardness increases as the atomic number increases from left to right across the period. Lanthanides have a high melting and boiling point, and they are extremely reactive. The lanthanides react readily with most nonmetals. Generally, they lose three outer electrons to form bonds with nonmetal atoms. They react with water and weak acids and burn easily in air.

The lanthanides and their compounds have many uses. Some are useful catalysts, speeding up chemical reactions in the petroleum industry. Others are used to make lasers and fluorescent lamps. They are also used in televisions, in the screen coatings that provide colored images. Some lanthanides are mixed with other metals to make alloys. The lanthanide metal adds to the strength of the final alloy. Some rare earths also have magnetic properties that are useful at extremely low temperatures where other magnetic elements do not work.

The actinide elements

The actinide elements are dense, radioactive metals. Over time, their atoms break down to form the atoms of other elements. Some are very unstable and will only form compounds with elements that increase their stability. Like most metals, the actinides react with weak acids to release hydrogen. This gas is also given

Tho-Radia beauty products were sold in France in the 1930s. They contained thorium, a radioactive rare-earth element, and radium, a radioactive alkaline-earth element. Both were once thought to be beneficial to health!

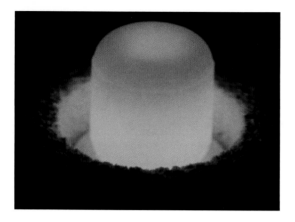

This pellet of plutonium glows with radioactivity. Plutonium forms as part of the decay process of uranium. Plutonium is used as a fuel source for space probes and in nuclear power plants. It is highly toxic and dangerous even at very low quantities.

off when the actinides are placed in boiling water. The actinides react readily with oxygen in the air, which discolors the metal with a thin layer of metal oxide.

Uranium is the most common element of the actinides and is widely distributed around the world. It usually occurs as an oxide, uranium dioxide, UO_2. As the most abundant radioactive element, uranium is mined and processed for use in the nuclear power industry. Some uranium is also used to make a luminous yellow-green glass. Thorium also occurs in many parts of the world in the mineral monazite and may be even more common than uranium. Thorium is mainly used in the making of mantles for gas lamps, but also has uses as a catalyst in the production of nitric and sulfuric acids and in the oil industry. Thorium, too, has potential for use as a nuclear fuel. The other actinide elements have limited uses. Plutonium is used to power heart pacemakers and in the nuclear industry. Americium is used in smoke detectors.

Building the actinides

Only the first four elements in the actinide series occur in any significant quantity in nature. These are actinium, thorium, protactinium, and uranium. Actinides with an atomic number greater than 92

(uranium) are known as the transuranium elements. Of these, only neptunium and plutonium have been found in nature, and even then only in trace amounts. All the other transuranium elements are synthetic elements made in the laboratory.

In 1940, American physicists Edwin McMillan (1907–1991) and Philip Abelson (1913–2004) produced an element with the atomic number 93. They named the element neptunium. A year later U.S. chemist Glenn T. Seaborg (1912–1999) and his colleagues produced element 94, named plutonium. In 1944, after more transuranium elements were discovered, Seaborg suggested that these elements should form a group similar to the lanthanide series. He called the new group the actinide series and placed both the lanthanides and actinides in a block at the bottom of the periodic table. Seaborg's revision was the last major change to the layout of the table.

Glenn Theodore Seaborg

Glenn Theodore Seaborg was born in Ishpeming, Michigan, on April 19, 1912. When he was a child, the family moved to Los Angeles. Seaborg studied at the University of California, Los Angeles (UCLA). He graduated in 1934 with a degree in chemistry. He then did postgraduate studies at the University of California, Berkeley. There, he studied with some of the leading scientists of the day, including American chemist Gilbert Lewis (1875–1946). Seaborg's research continued at Berkeley. Eventually, he became professor of chemistry.

It was during World War II (1939–1945) that Seaborg made his mark on the periodic table. In addition to plutonium, Seaborg discovered the elements americium, curium, berkelium, californium, einsteinium, fermium, mendelevium, and nobelium. In recognition of his contribution to chemistry, Seaborg shared the 1951 Nobel Prize with Edwin McMillan (1907–1991). Seaborg died in 1999, following complications after a stroke. The element seaborgium (106) is named in his honor.

When radioactive plutonium decays, it generates heat that can be used to create electricity. These radioactive thermoelectric generators are installed on spacecraft to power them during long missions.

End of the periodic table

The search for even heavier elements than seaborgium has continued since the 1970s. Much of the work has been carried out at laboratories in Darmstadt in Germany, Dubna in Russia, and Berkeley in California. Because these elements do not occur naturally they have to be created.

The key to the process of making a new element lies in the ratio of protons and neutrons in the nucleus of an atom. If the ratio is not correct, the nucleus becomes unstable and the atom breaks apart. Certain combinations of protons and neutrons are very stable and are called "magic" numbers. The most stable heavy element in nature is lead, with 82 protons and 126 neutrons. Beyond this ideal ratio, researchers have predicted other combinations of protons and neutrons that could result in new "superheavy" elements. Researchers prepare them by bombarding one heavy element, such as americium or curium, with another rich in neutrons. That starts a fusion reaction that begins a radioactive decay chain. The presence of the new element is detected by analyzing the products that form. Using this method the elements bohrium (107), hassium (108), meitnerium (109), darmstadtium (110), roentgenium (111), and copernicium (112) have been discovered.

Some researchers claim to have detected evidence that elements up to number 118 may have formed during experiments. However, their existence has not yet been proven.

In theory, chemists think that the maximum atomic number possible (the number of protons the nucleus can hold) lies somewhere between 170 and 210. However, it is doubtful whether chemists will actually identify such a large number of elements. The laws of science do not rule out the possibility of 210 protons in an atom, but the stability of the nucleus does. In fact, chemists may be close to finding all the elements of the periodic table. They think the maximum atomic number is about 120, which means there are eight or so new elements left to be discovered.

GLOSSARY

Absolute zero The lowest theoretically possible temperature, –459.67°F (–273.15°C).

Activation energy The difference between the average energy of reactant molecules at a given temperature and the energy they need to react.

Acid A compound that contains large amounts of hydrogen (H$^+$) ions.

Alkali A compound that contains large amounts of hydroxide (OH$^-$) ions.

Alloy A mixture of two or more metals or a metal and a nonmetal, such as carbon.

Atom The smallest unit of an element.

Atomic mass The number of protons and neutrons in a nucleus.

Atomic number The number of protons in an atom's nucleus.

Boiling point The temperature at which a liquid turns into a gas.

Bond An attraction between atoms.

By-product A substance that is produced when another material is made.

Catalyst An element or compound that helps a chemical reaction occur more quickly, but that is not altered by the reaction.

Chemical formula A combination of chemical symbols that shows the type and number of elements in a molecule. H$_2$O is the formula for water, which contains two hydrogen (H) atoms and one oxygen (O).

Chemical reaction A process in which atoms of different elements join or break apart.

Chemical symbol Letters used to represent a certain element, such as O for oxygen or Na for sodium.

Compound A substance formed when the atoms of two or more different elements bond together.

Conductive Describes a substance that carries electricity and heat well.

Conductor A substance that carries electricity and heat well.

Covalent bond A bond in which atoms share some of their electrons.

Density A measure of how tightly atoms are packed into a solid.

Ductile Describes a solid that can be drawn into long wires without breaking.

Earth's crust The layer of solid rock that covers the surface of Earth.

Electricity A stream of charged particles moving through a substance.

Electron shell A layer of electrons that surrounds the nucleus of an atom.

Element The simplest type of substance made up of just one type of atom.

Energy The ability to cause a change in something by heating it up, altering its shape, or making it move.

Group A column of related elements in the periodic table.

Half-life The amount of time it takes for half the isotopes in a sample to break down.

Inhibitor A substance that slows down a chemical reaction without being used up by it; also called a negative catalyst.

Insoluble A substance that cannot dissolve.

Insulator A substance that does not carry an electric current or heat.

Ion An atom that has lost or gained an electron or electrons.

Ionic bond A bond produced when oppositely charged ions are attracted to each other.

Kelvin scale The temperature scale that uses kelvins (K) as the unit of temperature, and where zero (0K) equals absolute zero (–459.67°F; –273.15°C).

Malleable Describes a material that can be bent easily or pounded into a flat sheet, such as many metals.

Melting point The temperature at which a solid substance melts into a liquid.

Metal A hard but flexible element. Metals are good conductors. Their atoms have only a few outer electrons.

Metallic bond A bond between a group of metal atoms that are sharing a pool of electrons.

Metalloid A substance with the properties of both a metal and a nonmetal.

Mineral A naturally occurring compound, such as those that make up rocks and soil.

Molecule Two or more atoms that are connected together.

Noble gases A group of gases that rarely react with other elements.

Nonmetal An element that is not a metal or metalloid. Nonmetals are poor conductors and their atoms tend to have several outer electrons.

Nucleus The central core of an atom containing protons and neutrons.

Ore A naturally occurring substance that contains valuable amounts of a metal.

Oxidation state A number used to describe how many electrons an atom has lost or gained.

Period A row of elements arranged across the periodic table.

Periodic table A table that organizes all the chemical elements into a simple chart according to the physical and chemical properties of their atoms. The elements are arranged by atomic number from 1 to 116.

Radioactive When an atom has an unstable nucleus that breaks apart.

Radioactive decay When small particles break off from an unstable nucleus.

Radioactivity The release of energy that results when the nucleus of an atom breaks down by fission or fusion.

Reaction rate The rate at which the concentrations of reactants and products change during the reaction.

Refine To purify a metal by removing unwanted elements.

Salt A compound made from positive and negative ions that forms when an alkali reacts with an acid.

Semiconductor A substance that conducts only in certain conditions.

Standard conditions Normal room temperature and pressure.

Transuranium elements Elements with an atomic number greater than that of uranium, which is 92.

Valence A measure of the number of bonds an atom can form with other atoms.

Valence electrons The outermost electrons in the shells of an atom, which are involved in chemical reactions.

FURTHER RESEARCH

Books

Atkins, P. W. *The Periodic Kingdom: A Journey into the Land of Chemical Elements.* New York, NY: Barnes & Noble Books, 2007.

Bendick, J., and Wiker, B. *The Mystery of the Periodic Table (Living History Library).* Bathgate, ND: Bethlehem Books, 2003.

Berg, J. *Biochemistry.* New York, NY: W. H. Freeman, 2006.

Brown, T. E. *et al. Chemistry: The Central Science.* Englewood Cliffs, NJ: Prentice Hall, 2008.

Cobb, C., and Fetterolf, M. L. *The Joy of Chemistry: The Amazing Science of Familiar Things.* Amherst, NY: Prometheus Books, 2010.

Davis, M. *et al. Modern Chemistry.* New York, NY: Holt, 2008.

Gray, Theodore. *Theo Gray's Mad Science: Experiments You Can Do at Home—But Probably Shouldn't.* New York, NY: Black Dog & Leventhal Publishers, 2009.

Greenberg A. *From Alchemy to Chemistry in Picture and Story.* Hoboken, NJ: Wiley, 2007.

Herr, N., and Cunningham, J. *Hands-on Chemistry Activities with Real-life Applications.* Hoboken, NJ: Jossey-Bass, 2002.

Karukstis, K. K., and Van Hecke, G. R. *Chemistry Connections: The Chemical Basis of Everyday Phenomena.* Burlington, MA: Academic Press, 2003.

Lehninger, A., Cox, M., and Nelson, D. *Lehninger's Principles of Biochemistry.* New York, NY: W. H. Freeman, 2008.

LeMay, E. *et al. Chemistry: Connections to Our Changing World.* New York, NY: Prentice Hall (Pearson Education), 2002.

Levere, T. H. *Transforming Matter: A History of Chemistry from Alchemy to the Buckyball.* Baltimore, MD: The Johns Hopkins University Press, 2001.

Oxlade, C. *Elements and Compounds (Chemicals in Action).* Chicago, IL: Heinemann, 2008.

Poynter, M. *Marie Curie: Discoverer of Radium (Great Minds of Science).* Berkeley Heights, NJ: Enslow Publishers, 2007.

Saunders, N. *Fluorine and the Halogens.* Chicago, IL: Heinemann Library, 2005.

Shevick, E., and Wheeler, R. *Great Scientists in Action: Early Life, Discoveries, and Experiments.* Carthage, IL: Teaching & Learning Company, 2004.

Stwertka, A. *A Guide to the Elements.* New York, NY: Oxford University Press, 2002.

Thompson, B. T. *Illustrated Guide to Home Chemistry Experiments: All Lab, No Lecture.* Sebastopol, CA: O'Reilly Media, 2008.

Tiner, J. H. *Exploring the World of Chemistry: From Ancient Metals to High-speed Computers.* Green Forest, AZ: Master Books, 2000.

Trombley, L., and Williams, F. *Mastering the Periodic Table: 50 Activities on the Elements.* Portland, ME: Walch, 2002.

Walker, P., and Wood, E. *Crime Scene Investigations: Real-life Science Labs for Grades 6–12.* Hoboken, NJ: Jossey-Bass, 2002.

Wilbraham, A., *et al. Chemistry.* New York, NY: Prentice Hall (Pearson Education), 2001.

Woodford, C., and Clowes, M. *Routes of Science: Atoms and Molecules.* San Diego, CA: Blackbirch Press, 2004.

Web sites

The Art and Science of Bubbles
www.sdahq.org/sdakids/bubbles
Information and activities about bubbles.

Chemical Achievers
www.chemheritage.org/classroom/chemach/index.html
Biographical details about leading chemists and their discoveries.

The Chemistry of Fireworks
library.thinkquest.org/15384/chem/chem.htm
Information on the chemical reactions that occur when a firework explodes.

Chemistry: The Periodic Table Online
www.webelements.com
Detailed information about elements.

Chemistry Tutor
library.thinkquest.org/2923
A series of Web pages that help with chemistry assignments.

Chem4Kids
www.chem4Kids.com
Includes sections on matter, atoms, elements, and biochemistry.

Chemtutor Elements
www.chemtutor.com/elem.htm
Information on a selection of the elements.

Eric Weisstein's World of Chemistry
scienceworld.wolfram.com/chemistry
Chemistry information divided into eight broad topics, from chemical reactions to quantum chemistry.

General Chemistry Help
chemed.chem.purdue.edu/genchem
General information on chemistry plus movie clips of key concepts.

IUPAC
www.iupac.org/
Web site of the International Union of Pure and Applied Chemistry.

Molecular Models
chemlabs.uoregon.edu/GeneralResources/models/models.html
A site that explains the use of molecular models.

New Scientist
www.newscientist.com/home.ns
Online science magazine providing general news on scientific developments.

The Physical Properties of Minerals
mineral.galleries.com/minerals/physical.htm
Methods for identifying minerals.

Scientific American
www.sciam.com
Latest news on developments in science and technology.

Virtual Laboratory: Ideal Gas Laws
zebu.uoregon.edu/nsf/piston.html
University of Oregon site showing simulation of ideal gas laws.

INDEX